1 JOHN
GALATIANS

EXPOSING RELIGIOUS COUNTERFEITS

PROJECT ENGINEER: Lyman Coleman,
Serendipity House

WRITERS FOR NOTES: Richard Peace,
William Cutler

WRITERS OF GROUP QUESTIONS:
Brenda Spoelstra, Andrew Sloan,
Lyman Coleman, Denny Rydberg,
Bill Tucker, John T. Anderson, John Crosby

TYPESETTING: Sharon Penington,
Maurice Lydick, John Winson,
Douglas LaBudde

PUBLISHER: Serendipity House is a
resource community specializing in the
equipping of pastors and church leaders for
small group ministry in the local church in
the English speaking world. A list of training
events and resources can be obtained by
writing to the address below.

SERENDIPITY GROUP BIBLE STUDY

Serendipity House / P.O.Box 1012 / Littleton, CO 80160

TOLL FREE 1-800-525-9563

97 98 99 / **301GBS series•CHG** / 6 5 4 3 2 1

Questions And Answers About
Starting a Bible Study Group

PURPOSE	1. *What is the purpose of a Bible study group?* Three things (and all three are important):
	a. Nurture—to be fed by God and grow in Christ, principally through Bible Study.
	b. Support—getting to know each other in a deeper way and caring for each other's needs.
	c. Mission—reaching out to non-churched people who are open to studying the Bible and reaching beyond your initial number until you can split into two groups ... and keep multiplying.
NON-CHURCHED	2. *How can people who don't go to church be interested in studying the Bible?* Pretty easy. In a recent survey, the Gallup Poll discovered that 74% of the people in America are looking for a spiritual faith.
TURNED-OFF	3. *Then, why don't they go to church?* Because they have a problem with the institutional church.
SEEKERS	4. *What are you suggesting?* That you start a Bible study group for these kinds of people.
	• People who are turned off by the church but are looking for a spiritual faith.
	• People who are struggling with personal problems and need a support group.
	• People who are crippled by a bad experience with the church and want to start over in their spiritual pilgrimage.
	• People who are down on themselves and need encouragement to see beyond their own shortcomings.
	• People who are looking for hope in the face of seemingly insurmountable difficulties.
	• People who flashed across your mind as you read over this list.

RECRUITING	5. *How do I get started?* Make a list of the "honest seekers you know" and keep this list on your refrigerator until you have asked everyone.
FIRST MEETING	6. *What do we do at the first meeting?* Decide on your group covenant—a "contract" that spells out your expectations and rules (see the center section, page C5).
DEVELOPING A CONTRACT	7. *How do we develop a contract?* Discuss these questions and ask someone to write down what you agree upon (This "contract" will be used again at the close to evaluate your group). • What is the purpose of our group? • What are the specific goals? • How long are we going to meet? (We recommend 6 to 12 weeks. Then if you wish to continue, you can renew the contract). • Where are we going to meet? • What is going to be the starting and ending time at the sessions? • What about babysitting/refreshments, etc.?
LIFECYCLE	8. *How long should a Bible study group last?* This should be taken in stages. (See flow chart below)
SHORT-TERM COMMITMENT	9. *Why only a few weeks to start with?* Because people will give priority to something if they know it's not for long. And they can always renew and keep going if they wish.

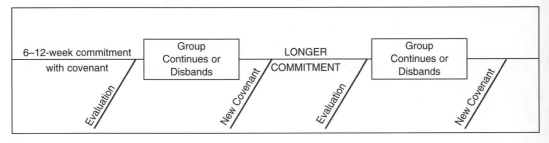

STUDY PLANS	**10.** *How do we go about the study of this book of the Bible?* This should be decided at the first meeting. Inside the front cover of this book are a number of options that you can choose from. You need to discuss these options and agree on your study plans.
HOMEWORK	**11.** *Is there any homework?* No—unless you want to do some research about a particular concern. If you are studying one of the longer books of the Bible, where you do not have time to cover every passage, you may want to combine units as suggested in "Course Options" and answer only one set of questions.
BIBLE IGNORANCE	**12.** *What if we have people in the group who know nothing about the Bible?* Great. This is what this group is all about. There are NOTES on the opposite page to refer to if you have any questions about a word, historical fact or significant person in the passage.
NOTES	**13.** *Who wrote these Notes?* Richard Peace, a Professor at Gordon Conwell Seminary and a recognized Bible scholar.
SERENDIPITY	**14.** *What is Serendipity?* A small research foundation that specializes in programs for support groups in a Christian context.
DREAM	**15.** *What is your dream?* Christian support groups for hurting and struggling people inside and outside of the church—built around a study of Scripture and care for one another. For further information, we invite you to call: TOLL FREE 1-800-525-9563, IN COLORADO 303-798-1313.

Introduction to

1 JOHN

John was an old man when he wrote his first epistle. All the other disciples were dead. Only he remained of the original Twelve. His long life had afforded him the opportunity to witness the spectacular growth of the church. It had begun with only a handful of disciples clustered together in Jerusalem. Now it had spread throughout the known world, and the believers had become so numerous that it was difficult to number them all.

But not all that John had seen was good. As well as growth, there had been dissension, defection, and heresy—even in the churches John pastored. In fact, this is why he came to write this epistle: a group of people from his church had gotten involved in strange doctrine. They had then left the church and formed their own community. Now they were trying to persuade other Christians to do the same thing—to leave and join this new group.

So John was compelled to write this letter. In fact, it had become an urgent need. Soon, like the other apostles, his time would be at an end. And when he was gone, who would ensure that the church remained loyal to the teachings of Jesus? It was vital that the church understand clearly what lay at the heart of Christianity. It was vital that Christians grasp firmly the nature of the Gospel.

So John wrote his first epistle. In it one gets the sense that here is John boiling down the Gospel to its essence: "God is Light; God is Love; Jesus is the Messiah, the Son of God who has come in the flesh; and we are to be his children who have eternal life, who do not continue in sin, and who love one another." This is what it is all about. This is what God has been trying to teach the human race for all these hundreds of years. Here is John distilling all the wisdom and insight of his long years into a few incisive chapters. In the First Epistle of John, therefore, what we have is essential Christianity as seen by the last of the Twelve. John records here his final thoughts on the nature of the faith so that, once and for all, we would get it straight. As such, John's epistle is the summation of revelation history and thus it is a book to master—with both heart and head.

Occasion

There were problems in John's church—deep ones that compelled him to write. It is difficult, of course, to reconstruct with full accuracy just what the situation was in the multiple house churches in the Ephesus area where John ministered. Still, it appears that what happened was that a group of Christians got involved in false teaching, split off from the church (2:19), and then started hassling their former friends, probably trying to convince them to espouse their new, "advanced" religious views (2:26). (This is a typical response. If you can get others to agree with your newly embraced viewpoint, then you yourself feel more confident that you are, indeed, "right.") Thus John writes this epistle to refute these erroneous views and to encourage those in the church to remain faithful to the Gospel as taught by the apostles.

The error of these secessionists was twofold: they had a defective view of Jesus and a wrong view of sin. On their view of Jesus, they were so caught up with the idea of Jesus as the divine, pre-existent Lord that they almost totally neglected his human side. While they probably would not deny that Jesus was a man, to them this fact was insignificant. His humanity did not really matter in comparison with his divinity. As a result, they did not believe Jesus to be the Messiah (2:22; 5:1). In particular, they denied that Jesus, as the Son of God, had died. This was the really fatal error, because it cuts to the very heart of the Gospel. Since God is love and since love is the laying down of one's life (John 15:13), if the Son of God did not die then God has not been revealed in Christ.

They also had an erroneous view of ethics. Specifically, they claimed to be free from sin, and free from the commandment to love others. Since they did not confess that Jesus was the Messiah, they did not feel any need to obey what he said. And since they felt that they were free from sin, they did not need the Son of God to die in their place for their sins.

These secessionists had come to think of themselves as some sort of spiritual "elite," claiming (probably by direct revelation—see 4:1–6) that they had a "deeper" understanding of Christianity than others. As an antidote to this sort of spiritual pride, John reminds his readers again and again that Christians are called upon to love one another. They are not to look down on those brothers and sisters who do not measure up to their own (supposed) superior insight.

It is not clear what, if any, "label" can be affixed to this group of secessionists. The ideas they held were probably related to what later became Gnosticism—a philosophy that taught that matter (including the body) was impure and that "spirit" was all that really counted. Therefore, it is not surprising that these secessionists, with this Gnostic view of reality, minimized the humanity of Jesus. To them salvation came via illumination. Thus esoteric "knowledge" is what they sought, instead of hearing and heeding apostolic doctrine.

Authorship

But did the apostle John actually write this epistle? This has been the assumption thus far in these notes. Yet there are those scholars who would question whether this is so.

In fact, the author of this letter is nowhere named in 1 John. So, whatever one concludes, it is by way of speculation. However, a good case can be made that John, the beloved apostle, is indeed the author of this epistle. There are a number of reasons for attributing this anonymous epistle to him, including:

1. The strong tradition dating back to the early days of the Church that John was the author.
2. The many similarities in style and content between the Gospel of John and this epistle. The same sharp contrasts appear in both—between light and darkness; truth and falsehood; love and hate. What differences do exist between the two books can be traced to differences in purpose arising out of differences in audi-

ence, since the historical context had shifted between the time of the Gospel and the time of this epistle.
3. The internal information in the epistle points to John as the author. For example, the author tells us that he was one of the original eyewitnesses of Jesus (1:1–2). Also, the author writes with the air of authority that would be expected of one who was an apostle (see 4:6).

Date

It is very difficult to fix a date to this epistle. The evidence is not clear nor conclusive. However, the best guess is that 1 John was written toward the end of the New Testament era (A.D. 90-95), by which time this gnostic-like heresy had begun to flourish.

Style

1 John is written in the simplest Greek found in all the New Testament. (It is the first book seminary students learn to translate.) 5,437 different Greek words appear in the New Testament, yet in the three Johannine epistles, only 303 of these are used—5 1/2 percent of the total. This is not to say, however, that 1 John is a simple, superficial book. On the contrary, it is one of the most profound books in the entire New Testament. Perhaps because of (not despite) his simple vocabulary, John focuses in on the core of the Gospel. All else is cut away. He writes only what really matters.

A story is told by Jerome about the "blessed John the evangelist" when he was an extremely old man. According to Jerome, John now has to be carried into the worship service at Ephesus. John is unable to say anything except "little children, love one another," which he repeats over and over. The believers, having heard this same thing so often, ask: "Master, why do you always say this?" "Because," he replied, "it is enough."

Martin Luther wrote: "I have never read a book written in simpler words than this one, and yet the words are inexpressible."

Literary Form

1 John is not an epistle in the sense that 2 and 3 John are (or in the sense of Paul's letters). It does not identify the writer or the recipients. In fact, there is no specific name or place mentioned anywhere in this document. There is no salutation nor is there a final greeting. It is clear that this is intentional, since John knew perfectly well how a letter was written. 3 John has been called by some the most perfect example in the New Testament of Greek letter format. Clearly, here John was writing a different sort of document.

Three things are evident about John's effort here. First, this is a literary document. John states some 13 times that he is writing (in contrast to speaking or preaching; see, for example, 1:4). And, second, it is clear that he has a specific audience in mind, which he refers to as "you" (in the plural) some 22 times. Third, there is a so-called "doubled-opening" (similar to that in James), within which John states twice the themes he then develops in the rest of the manuscript. So what we have here is probably a "literary epistle"—a written document addressed to a particular audience. His audience is the community of churches in and around Ephesus that he pastored and which remained loyal to the Gospel he preached.

Structure and Theme

It is difficult to "outline" 1 John; i.e., to track the flow of the author's thought and put it into neat categories and divisions (as one can do with Romans, for example). Rather, it seems that John (much like James) would write a paragraph and then be reminded of a related topic which he would then deal with in the next paragraph. This, in turn, would spark a further thought. This is not to say that John's ideas tumble out in a haphazard fashion. This is certainly not the case. His ideas are focused and interrelated. The ideas hang together—but not by means of a western style of logic. The structure is almost spiral, "for the development of a theme often brings us back almost to the starting-point; almost but not quite, for there is a slight shift which provides a transition to a fresh theme; or it may be to a theme which had apparently been dismissed at an earlier point and now comes up for consideration from a slightly different angle" (Dodd).

John's central concern is quite clear, however. He wants to define the marks of a true Christian, over against what was being taught by the secessionists. This is very important. He wants his congregation to have the assurance that they do, indeed, have eternal life (5:13), despite what the false teachers are saying. What, then, are these "marks"? According to John Stott, the characteristics of a true Christian in 1 John are these: right belief (the doctrinal test), righteousness (the moral test), and love (the social test).

UNIT 1—The Word of Life / 1 John 1:1–4

Scripture

The Word of Life

1 *That which was from the beginning, which we have heard, which we have seen with our eyes, which we have looked at and our hands have touched—this we proclaim concerning the Word of life. ²The life appeared; we have seen it and testify to it, and we proclaim to you the eternal life, which was with the Father and has appeared to us. ³We proclaim to you what we have seen and heard, so that you also may have fellowship with us. And our fellowship is with the Father and with his Son, Jesus Christ. ⁴We write this to make our*ᵃ *joy complete.*

Group Questions

Every group meeting has three goals: **(1) To Begin** (15 minutes) to break the ice; **(2) Read Scripture and Discuss** (30 Minutes); and **(3) To Close and Pray** (15–30 Minutes). Try to keep on schedule. The most important time is the prayer time.

TO BEGIN / 15 Minutes (Choose 1 or 2)

❏ Where were you living when you were 7 years old?
❏ What was your house like at age 7? What do you remember about your room?
❏ Who was a very special person in your life then?

READ SCRIPTURE AND DISCUSS / 30 Minutes

❏ When have you been part of a group where you enjoyed true fellowship—where there was mutual love and understanding?
❏ John makes a point of saying that he has heard, seen and touched Jesus. What were your "beginnings" with Jesus like? In what ways have you "seen", "heard" and "touched" him?
❏ There was a serious problem in John's church: a group had split off and were teaching that Jesus did not really die. They also believed they were without sin. What could not be proclaimed if Jesus hadn't died (v. 2)? Have you ever come close to losing your faith in Christ? What happened?
❏ What emotion will John experience when he makes clear the truth of Jesus (v. 4)?
❏ Who has been like the apostle John in your life—a person who has convinced you of Jesus' love and cared about your spiritual growth?
❏ Why did you decide to join this Bible study group? What are you hoping to get out of this group?

TO CLOSE AND PRAY / 15–30 Minutes

❏ What "season" are you experiencing in your spiritual life right now? Spring—life is beginning to bud? Winter—the days have been cold and dark? Fall—some days beautiful, some with a chill in the air?
❏ What would you like this group to discuss about the coming weeks together (consider study, prayer, shared leadership, outreach, confidentiality, accountability, etc.)? In order to get the most out of 1 John, what will you put into it?
❏ Who do you know who might like to join this group next week?
❏ How would you like this group to pray for you in the coming week?

ᵃ4 Some manuscripts *your*

Notes

1:1–4 John begins his letter with a prologue that is reminiscent of the prologue to his Gospel (John 1:1–18). Both prologues focus on the pre-existent Word of God who has been revealed to humanity. But there are also differences between the two. In the Gospel prologue, the emphasis is on the divine nature of the Word. In this prologue, the emphasis is on the *physical manifestation* of the Word of God. This difference is due to the difference in audiences. In his Gospel, John wrote to Jews who did not believe that God could reveal himself in the person of Jesus. But here, the secessionists presuppose that Jesus is the Son of God. Their problem is that they neglect his human side. This is why John emphasizes the fact that the pre-existent Word has been experienced by auditory, visual, and manual means. Although this prologue is only four verses long, it is a complex piece of writing. In Greek, this is a single sentence which is, according to one scholar, a "grammatical tangle" (Dodd). The structure has a distinct purpose—John focuses attention on the object which is proclaimed (Jesus Christ), rather than on the act of proclamation itself.

1:1 Although this document lacks the usual identification of sender and recipient (as well as the normal greeting and prayer), it is clear that this is not an anonymous tract written to a general audience. Scattered throughout the letter are abundant personal comments and specific references (e.g., 2:19). **which.** John begins with four clauses, each introduced by "which." The first clause describes who the "Word of life" is. The next three describe how he was experienced. *from the beginning.* The initial clause makes the astonishing assertion that this "Word of life" was pre-existent (see John 1:1). Since only divine beings preexisted, John affirms Jesus' deity. *heard/seen/touched.* However, John's emphasis is on the human nature of Jesus. The next three clauses describe how his physical presence was experienced. Notice the progression: in the OT, men and women had *heard* God on many occasions; occasionally they had *seen* some aspect of God (see Ex. 3:1–6; 33:18–23); but no one had ever *touched* God. This was the final proof that the Word of life had indeed been "made flesh and dwelt among us" (John 1:14, KJV). In Greek courts, the testimony of two senses was required in order to verify that something occurred (Brown). John offers evidence from a third sense as well. *touched.* This word means literally "to feel after" or "to grope," as a blind person might do. It also means "to examine closely" (Brooke). *Word of*

life. The message preached by the apostles and by Jesus himself concerned eternal life (i.e., spiritual life). This is one sense of the phrase "Word of life." But Jesus not only preached this message. He *was* the message. This is the second sense of the phrase (see John 1:4; 11:25–26; 14:6).

1:2 This is a parenthesis in which John declares in unequivocal terms that *Jesus* is the Word he is talking about. *we.* The author is among those who knew Jesus personally. *testify.* This is a legal term describing what an eyewitness does while in court. Such a person makes a public declaration of what he or she has experienced firsthand. *the eternal life.* John focuses on what is so significant about Jesus: he is Life itself. God's very life has appeared in the historical person of Jesus (see John 1:2).

1:3 *we proclaim.* This is the main verb of the opening sentence. It clarifies the intention of the prologue. John's aim is to identify the nature of the apostolic proclamation, which is that Jesus is the incarnate God. *fellowship.* This word means literally, in Greek, "having in common." It has the dual sense of *participation together* in shared activity or outlook, and *union together* because of that shared experience. John's purpose is to bring others into participation and union with him and his colleagues, and thus into participation and union with the Father and the Son. *with the Father and with his Son.* Apparently the false teachers were saying that it was possible to have fellowship with God apart from Christ. John's point is that fellowship with God is possible only through Jesus (2:23), because in him eternal life (i.e., God's life) is manifested.

1:4 John identifies his second reason for writing. He wants his own joy to be completed. *joy.* This is the profound gladness or satisfaction that comes when one participates in the life of God. It is an important term for John. In this epistle he indicates that the joy which began with the experience of the resurrected Lord is brought to completion via the experience of this full-orbed fellowship between Father, Son, and the children of God. *complete.* Full, lacking nothing.

UNIT 2—Walking in the Light / 1 John 1:5–2:14

Scripture

Walking in the Light

*⁵ This is the message we have heard from him and declare to you: God is light; in him there is no darkness at all. ⁶If we claim to have fellowship with him yet walk in the darkness, we lie and do not live by the truth. ⁷But if we walk in the light, as he is in the light, we have fellowship with one another, and the blood of Jesus, his Son, purifies us from all*ᵃ *sin.*

⁸If we claim to be without sin, we deceive ourselves and the truth is not in us. ⁹If we confess our sins, he is faithful and just and will forgive us our sins and purify us from all unrighteousness. ¹⁰If we claim we have not sinned, we make him out to be a liar and his word has no place in our lives.

2 *My dear children, I write this to you so that you will not sin. But if anybody does sin, we have one who speaks to the Father in our defense—Jesus Christ, the Righteous One. ²He is the atoning sacrifice for our sins, and not only for ours but also for*ᵇ *the sins of the whole world.*

*³We know that we have come to know him if we obey his commands. ⁴The man who says, "I know him," but does not do what he commands is a liar, and the truth is not in him. ⁵But if anyone obeys his word, God's love*ᶜ *is truly made complete in him. This is how we know we are in him: ⁶Whoever claims to live in him must walk as Jesus did. ⁷Dear friends, I am not writing you a new command but an old one, which you have had since the beginning. This old command is the message you have heard. ⁸Yet I am writing you a new command; its truth is seen in him and you, because the darkness is passing and the true light is already shining.*

Group Questions

Every group meeting has three goals: **(1) To Begin** (15 minutes) to break the ice; **(2) Read Scripture and Discuss** (30 Minutes); and **(3) To Close and Pray** (15–30 Minutes). Try to keep on schedule. The most important time is the prayer time.

TO BEGIN / 15 Minutes (Choose 1 or 2)

❏ As a child, were you afraid of the dark? What "monsters" were in the dark that scared you?
❏ What game did you play as a child where you were blindfolded? What was the experience like?
❏ Growing up, who was the "realist" in your life—one who helped you understand "the way life really is"?

READ SCRIPTURE AND DISCUSS / 30 Minutes

❏ What characteristics of light reflect who God is? Has God brought light to your life? In what way? Or do you more often feel like you're "in the dark"?
❏ What false claims do John's opponents make (vv. 1:6,8)? How do you feel about the consistency of your own life? Do you feel more as if you're living the truth or living a lie? Why?
❏ What hope does John give when people fail to live in light of God's love (1:9; 2:1–2)?
❏ When you know you've sinned, how long does it take for you to confess? What is God's part and what is your part in the confession process?
❏ How can the command to love God and others (v. 2:7) be new and old at the same time? How is its truth seen in Jesus (think of examples from the Gospels)? Whom have you known as someone who models this behavior?
❏ What, then, are the two tests given in this passage for determining whether one really knows God (vv. 2:3,10)? How are you doing in each of these areas?
❏ What three things does John stress again in verses 2:12–13? Which one of these do you most need to hear this week?

[Scripture and questions continued on page 14]

ᵃ7 Or every   ᵇ2 Or He is the one who turns aside God's wrath, taking away our sins, and not only ours but also   ᶜ5 Or word, love for God

Notes

1:5–2:2 John examines the barrier that prevents such fellowship (i.e., sin) and how to deal with it.

1:5 God is light. John's second great assertion about God (the first being that *God had come in the flesh*—vv. 1–3). In the Bible, "light" was connected on the intellectual level with truth, and on the moral level with purity.

1:6 If we claim. The first of three false claims that John will refute. He will measure the validity of each against the apostolic proclamation that God is light and in him is no darkness. **to have fellowship ... yet walk in the darkness.** It is claimed by the false teachers that it is possible to be in union with God and yet habitually sin. But if God is *light,* then by definition, those who walk in *darkness* cannot be part of him. This was a common error. It was felt that since the body was insignificant, it did not matter what a person did. The true essence of the person—the "spirit"—remained untouched and thus uncontaminated by sin.

1:7 walk in the light. The image here is of a person confidently striding forth, illuminated by the light of God's truth, in contrast to the person who stumbles around in darkness. **purifies.** If the first result of "walking in the light" is fellowship with one another, the second result is cleansing from sin. The verb tense indicates that this purification occurs not just once, but is a continuous process.

1:8 If we claim to be without sin. The second false claim: that they are sinless. It is one thing to deny that sin breaks fellowship with God (as in vv. 6–7). At least then the existence of sin is admitted (even if its impact is denied); but it is another thing to deny the fact of sin altogether.

1:9 If we confess our sins. After naming the problem, John states the antidote. Rather than denying their sinful natures, they need to admit their sin to God and so gain forgiveness. **just.** The granting of forgiveness is not merely an act of unanticipated mercy but a response of justice, since the conditions for forgiveness have been fulfilled as a result of the death of Christ.

1:10 If we claim we have not sinned. The third false claim: not only do they say that at the present moment they are without sin (v. 8), they actually claim never to have sinned! The false teachers might admit that sin does break fellowship with God (v. 6) and that all people have an inborn sinful nature (v. 8), but they would still deny that they, in fact, have ever actually sinned. **we make him out to be a liar.** By claiming sinlessness they are, in essence, saying that God is lying about human nature and about his claim to forgive people.

2:1 anybody does sin. While urging sinlessness as a goal to strive for, John knows that in this present life this cannot be achieved. So the issue then is how to deal with sin. The answer is found in the triple role of Jesus as the advocate, the righteous one, and the atoning sacrifice. **one who speaks ... in our defense.** Since people have no basis on which to ask for forgiveness, Jesus does so on their behalf. **Righteous One.** Jesus is righteous, both in the sense of being an example to follow and, especially, in the sense of not being contaminated by personal sin.

2:2 the atoning sacrifice. Jesus, the advocate, bases his plea (that their sin should be forgiven) on the fact of his death to pay for their sin. Such a sacrifice is effective because he himself was without sin, and so could take the place of another.

2:3–11 John now addresses his own flock, exhorting them to follow God's commands. He identifies two "tests" by which people can be certain they actually know God: the test of obedience and the test of love. Those who truly know God live in his way and love as Jesus loved.

2:3 have come to know him. Previously John has spoken about *having fellowship with God* (see 1:3,6,7). Now he speaks about the parallel concept, that of *knowing God* (see 2:4,13,14; 3:6,16; 4:16). The verb tense indicates that he is thinking about a past experience ("we have come to know him"). **if we obey his commands.** The first test as to whether a person knows God, therefore, is moral in nature: does that person keep God's commands? To know God is to live in his way. The false teachers claim to know God but, as John will show, they live in a way that belies that claim.

[Notes continued on page 15]

Scripture (Continued)

⁹*Anyone who claims to be in the light but hates his brother is still in the darkness. ¹⁰Whoever loves his brother lives in the light, and there is nothing in him^d to make him stumble. ¹¹But whoever hates his brother is in the darkness and walks around in the darkness; he does not know where he is going, because the darkness has blinded him.*

¹²*I write to you, dear children,*
because your sins have been forgiven
on account of his name.
¹³*I write to you, fathers,*
because you have known him who is
from the beginning.
I write to you, young men,
because you have overcome the evil
one.
I write to you, dear children,
because you have known the Father.
¹⁴*I write to you, fathers,*
because you have known him who is
from the beginning.
I write to you, young men,
because you are strong,
and the word of God lives in you,
and you have overcome the evil one.

Group Questions (Continued)

TO CLOSE AND PRAY / 15–30 Minutes

❑ If you were to give a spiritual "weather report" on your life over the last six months and over the last week, what would it be: Dark and stormy? Bright and cloudless sky? Partly cloudy? Dull, slate-gray and overcast? Why?
❑ How do you feel about opening up to this group? How can they help you?
❑ Did you invite anyone to join the group?
❑ What would you like the group to remember in prayer for you this week?

^d*10* Or *it*

14

Notes (Continued)

2:4 *does not do.* The emphasis here is on sins of omission (not doing), in contrast to 1:6, where the emphasis is on sins of commission (walking in darkness).

2:6 John introduces the idea of the "imitation of Christ." Christians are habitually to live the way Jesus lived. He is their model. As he walked, so should they walk. ***live in him.*** The third phrase which John uses to describe union with God. (In 1:3 he used the phrase "having fellowship with God," and in 2:3 he spoke about "knowing God.")

2:7–11 If the first test of whether one is actually a Christian is moral in nature (Do you obey God?), then the second test (given here) is relational in orientation (Do you love others?).

2:7–8 This is not a new command (v. 7), in that it is found in the OT (Lev. 19:18; Deut. 6:5) and taught by Jesus (Mark 12:28–31). It is *new* (v. 8) in the sense that Jesus tied together two previously separate commands (that of loving God and loving others) and broadened their application (Christians are to love everyone, not just those in their own group).

2:9–10 *light/love.* John here links sets of contrasting images: light and darkness with love and hate. Those who are in the light, love. Those who are in the darkness, hate. In other words, enlightenment goes hand in hand with active care for others.

2:11 *hates.* "Hate" is not an emotional response to others; it is the lack of loving deeds done on their behalf.

2:12 *children.* Some scholars feel that John is addressing the whole community by means of this term. ***have been forgiven.*** The verb tense indicates that John is thinking of the forgiveness that comes at the time of conversion, whereas in 1:9 his concern was with ongoing forgiveness for subsequent sins based on the confession of sins.

2:13 *fathers.* The spiritually mature in the congregation. ***young men.*** To be a Christian does not merely entail the enjoyment of sins forgiven and a warm relationship with God. It is also a vigorous battle against evil. ***overcome.*** In the same way that Christ overcame Satan via his death and resurrection, so too Christians are to overcome the evil one.

2:14 *word of God.* This is the source of this overcoming power. The "young men" know God's will and have lived in conformity to it. ***lives in you.*** The word of God is meant not only to be understood, but it is also intended to be incorporated into a person's very being.

UNIT 3—Do Not Love the World / Warning Against Antichrists / 1 John 2:15–27

Scripture

Do Not Love the World

[15]Do not love the world or anything in the world. If anyone loves the world, the love of the Father is not in him. [16]For everything in the world—the cravings of sinful man, the lust of his eyes and the boasting of what he has and does—comes not from the Father but from the world. [17]The world and its desires pass away, but the man who does the will of God lives forever.

Warning Against Antichrists

[18]Dear children, this is the last hour; and as you have heard that the antichrist is coming, even now many antichrists have come. This is how we know it is the last hour. [19]They went out from us, but they did not really belong to us. For if they had belonged to us, they would have remained with us; but their going showed that none of them belonged to us.
[20]But you have an anointing from the Holy One, and all of you know the truth.[a] *[21]I do not write to you because you do not know the truth, but because you do know it and because no lie comes from the truth. [22]Who is the liar? It is the man who denies that Jesus is the Christ. Such a man is the antichrist—he denies the Father and the Son. [23]No one who denies the Son has the Father; whoever acknowledges the Son has the Father also.*
[24]See that what you have heard from the beginning remains in you. If it does, you also will remain in the Son and in the Father. [25]And this is what he promised us—even eternal life.
[26]I am writing these things to you about those who are trying to lead you astray. [27]As for you, the anointing you received from him remains in you, and you do not need anyone to teach you. But as his anointing teaches you about all things and as that anointing is real, not counterfeit—just as it has taught you, remain in him.

[a]20 Some manuscripts *and you know all things*

Group Questions

Every group meeting has three goals: **(1) To Begin** (15 minutes) to break the ice; **(2) Read Scripture and Discuss** (30 Minutes); and **(3) To Close and Pray** (15–30 Minutes). Try to keep on schedule. The most important time is the prayer time.

TO BEGIN / 15 Minutes (Choose 1 or 2)

❏ What kind of disobedience do you remember as being the most tempting for you as a child? Lying? Hitting? Saying bad words?
❏ What was your parents' most common form of punishment when you disobeyed?
❏ Are you more likely today to err on the side of doing what you shouldn't or not doing what you should?

READ SCRIPTURE AND DISCUSS / 30 Minutes

❏ What does John mean by "the world" (vv. 15–16)? Is it wrong to love the outdoors, or your pet? Are all human desires contrary to God's will? Why?
❏ In what areas of your life does love for the world compete with love for God: In your use of money? Time? Priorities? Relationships? Ambitions?
❏ What is the anointing in verse 20? How does this anointing help a person to know and remain in the truth (vv. 20,24)? How do you sense the Holy Spirit's presence in your life? How do you need a greater sense of his presence?
❏ In what way are the antichrists in this passage foreshadowing the Antichrist to come? What danger do they pose to the church?
❏ What criteria can you use to distinguish between: (a) new insights into Christian truths that the Holy Spirit brings to light, and (b) new teachings that undermine the Christian faith?
❏ Why are there only two options in verse 23?
❏ What would you say to a friend who is excited about Jesus, but doesn't want to go to church? He claims there is hypocrisy in the church, and besides, he is filled with the Spirit and doesn't need other teachers. He just wants to be out there spreading the Gospel.

TO CLOSE AND PRAY / 15–30 Minutes

❏ On a scale of 1 to 10, with 1 being the world and 10 being God, where has your focus been over the last week? What has influenced your focus?
❏ How can this group support you in seeking the will of God rather than the desires of the world?
❏ What prayer requests would you like to share?

Notes

2:15–17 John warns his readers about an attitude that could bring them down, should they feel immune to the power of evil. The attitude they are to avoid is "love of the world." John bases his command on two factors: the incompatibility of love for God with love for the world (vv. 15–16), and the transience of worldly desires compared to the eternal life of those who do God's will (v. 17). John is attacking an attitude ("love of the world"). He is not attacking "things" *per se*, much less people.

2:15 love. The love which John speaks about is the act of caring, expressed by what a person does. As such, this "love" is appropriately directed toward God (v. 5) and toward others (v. 10), but not toward the pleasures of the world. **world.** That which is alienated from God and is, in fact, contrary to who God is. It refers to pagan culture which has abandoned God.

2:16 everything. Since God created the world (John 1:3), John cannot mean that everything in the world is automatically evil. In this verse, it is evident that what he had in mind are those aspects of the world which stand in opposition to God's ways. **cravings.** That part of human nature which demands gratification. **lust of the eyes.** Greed which is aroused by sight. A person sees something and wants it. **boasting.** Pride in one's possessions; an attitude of arrogance because one has acquired so much.

2:18–27 John returns to the question of distinguishing between those who are true Christians and those who are counterfeit. He adds a third test: the true Christian remains firmly committed to the truth of God. This is the doctrinal test (Stott).

2:18 antichrist. The incarnation of evil and Satan— just as Christ was the incarnation of good and God. **antichrists.** John notes that the Antichrist's coming was not some future threat. Even at that moment, the "spirit of the antichrist" (see 4:3) was loose in the world and active in those who deny Christ and his teachings (see v. 22).

2:19 they went out from us. John now identifies those who are imbued with the spirit of the Antichrist. It is none other than the successionists (false teachers) who left the church and seek to win over their former friends and colleagues to their point of view (see v. 26). **none of them belonged to us.** John distinguishes between the visible church (which consists of those who participate in church activities) and the invisible church (those who also belong to Christ). The two groups are not necessarily the same.

2:20 an anointing. Just as Jesus was anointed with the Holy Spirit (Luke 4:18), so too is the believer. The Holy Spirit is thus the one that guides the Christian into all truth (John 14:17; 15:26; 16:13).

2:21 John does not offer any "new truth" in this epistle. His aim is to reassure them (in the face of the claims being made by the successionists) that they already have the truth. **no lie comes from the truth.** John's reasoning is this: true Christians have the Holy Spirit and therefore know the truth (v. 20). Those who know the truth do not lie. Therefore, the implication is that those who are lying (by teaching false doctrine) do not know the truth because they do not have the Holy Spirit, and thus they are not true Christians.

2:22 John now reveals the major lie in the successionists' false teaching: they deny that Jesus is the Messiah and the Son of God.

2:23 denies/acknowledges. These are the only two options when it comes to Jesus. The idea here is of public confession and public denial.

2:24 remain. John's point is that when they remain in the truth they will remain in fellowship with God. To "remain" expresses a continuing relationship. The message must continue to be present and active in the lives of those who have heard it. They must continually call it to mind and let it affect their lives (Marshall).

2:27 remains in you. In verse 24, the stress was on the activity of Christians to ensure that they remained faithful to the Word of God. Here the complementary truth is expressed: by God's grace, Christians remain in this teaching. Human response and divine activity are both part of the Christian life. **teach.** John is not saying that after being anointed with the Holy Spirit, Christians need no more instruction. John is, in fact, instructing them via this letter! What they do not need is instruction by the false teachers. **all things.** This is not "everything that can be known," but rather "all that you need to know."

UNIT 4—Children of God / 1 John 2:28–3:10

Scripture

Children of God

²⁸And now, dear children, continue in him, so that when he appears we may be confident and unashamed before him at his coming. ²⁹If you know that he is righteous, you know that everyone who does what is right has been born of him.

3 *How great is the love the Father has lavished on us, that we should be called children of God! And that is what we are! The reason the world does not know us is that it did not know him. ²Dear friends, now we are children of God, and what we will be has not yet been made known. But we know that when he appears,ᵃ we shall be like him, for we shall see him as he is.*

³Everyone who has this hope in him purifies himself, just as he is pure. ⁴Everyone who sins breaks the law; in fact, sin is lawlessness. ⁵But you know that he appeared so that he might take away our sins. And in him is no sin. ⁶No one who lives in him keeps on sinning. No one who continues to sin has either seen him or known him.

⁷Dear children, do not let anyone lead you astray. He who does what is right is righteous, just as he is righteous. ⁸He who does what is sinful is of the devil, because the devil has been sinning from the beginning. The reason the Son of God appeared was to destroy the devil's work. ⁹No one who is born of God will continue to sin, because God's seed remains in him; he cannot go on sinning, because he has been born of God. ¹⁰This is how we know who the children of God are and who the children of the devil are: Anyone who does not do what is right is not a child of God; nor is anyone who does not love his brother.

Group Questions

TO BEGIN / 15 Minutes (Choose 1 or 2)

❏ Who would motivate you to clean your house (or your room)? The President? Your mother-in-law? An old friend?

❏ Who is the "neat freak" in your family? Are you more of a "neat freak" or a "messie"?

❏ Whom have you respected because of his or her clean living and high values? What stands out to you about this person?

READ SCRIPTURE AND DISCUSS / 30 Minutes

❏ What kind of feeling would you have if Jesus returned right now? Excited? Relieved? Ashamed?

❏ What tell-tale attitudes and actions characterize a person "born of God" (2:29; 3:1b,3,6,7,10)? As you get older, do you find it easier or harder to resist sinful desires? Why?

❏ What do verses 3:1–3 imply about God? What does this mean for our self-image? How have you experienced God's lavish love this week?

❏ How do verses 6 and 10 fit with 1:8? Are Christians sinless? Does John mean that Christians do not sin: At all? Habitually? Deliberately? Inadvertently? Or is he providing a gauge to evaluate teachers? Why do you think so?

❏ When have you experienced spiritual warfare? How did you deal with it? How can a Christian recognize and deal with our society's "whatever is right for you" attitude (moral relativism)?

❏ John says that the main source of tension between the world and Christians is conduct (or sin). Despite this tension, what must go hand-in-hand with obedience for a Christian (v. 10)? When has it recently been difficult for you to love?

TO CLOSE AND PRAY / 15–30 Minutes

❏ How clearly has your life mirrored God this week? Like a clear mountain lake? Like a rushing stream with occasional pools? Like pounding waves—not much space for God to be seen? Why?

❏ What would you like to work on this week in your relationship with God?

❏ How can this group pray for you?

ᵃ2 Or *when it is made known*

Notes

2:28–3:3 In the previous unit (2:18–27), John urged his readers to resist the proselytizing of the dissenters and to remain in Christ. In these verses he continues to urge his readers to remain in Christ, but now the reason he gives has to do with the second coming of Christ. If they remain in Christ, when they meet the Lord at the Second Coming they will not be ashamed. Instead, they will be confident before the Lord (2:28). Furthermore, they know that then they will see Christ as he is and be made like him (3:2). The Second Coming is thus a source of great hope for the Christian and an encouragement to holy living.

2:28 *confident and unashamed.* On the Day of Judgment those who have rejected Christ will feel a sense of unworthiness and shame in the presence of his holiness (see Isa. 6:5), and because of their open disgrace at having rejected Christ. In contrast, Christians will be able boldly to approach the royal presence because they have lived their lives in union with Christ. *his coming.* The Greek word *parousia* was used in secular literature to describe the visit of a ruler to a particular region of his kingdom. It carried with it the idea of great rejoicing and celebration.

2:29 *everyone who does what is right.* One consequence of spiritual rebirth is right living. It is, in fact, a sign of rebirth as the child begins to display the characteristics of his or her father. *born of him.* Thus far John has described Christians as those who "have fellowship with the Father and with his Son" (1:3), as those who "know God" (2:3,4,13,14), as those who are "in Christ" (2:5,6), as those who are "in the light" (2:9,10), and as those who "abide" in the Father and the Son (2:24,27,28). Now he offers yet another description of what it means to be a Christian. Christians are those who experience "spiritual rebirth." He thus defines the relationship between the believer and God by means of the analogy of the relationship between a child and a father. (See also 1 Peter 1:3,23; Titus 3:5.)

3:1 *The reason the world does not know us.* If the world knew God, it would recognize his children. But in fact this is not the case. The world hates God and so hates his children (see John 15:18–25). Such hostility is another sign that these believers are indeed his children.

3:3 Christians purify themselves in anticipation of Christ's return. *this hope.* Namely, that one day Christ will appear again (at which time they will see him as he really is and be changed, so as to become like him). *pure.* This is a common word in the Bible denoting the outward purity required of those persons or objects involved in temple worship. In the usage here it speaks of the moral purity (freedom from sinning) that is required of Christians. Such purification is necessary for those who are in union with Christ. The secessionists, in contrast, were not much concerned about sin (1:5–2:2).

3:5 John gives another reason for not sinning. The very purpose for Jesus to come in the first place was to take away sin. So it is obvious that Jesus stands over against sin. Furthermore, there was no sin in Jesus' life. The implication is that those who are in union with Christ will reflect this same abhorrence of sin. *in him is no sin.* John asserts that Jesus was sinless. His testimony is all the more powerful, since this is not his main point. This is merely an "aside." John is not trying to prove anything. He is simply stating what he knows to be true. And John was in a position to know whether Jesus was actually without sin because he lived with Jesus for some three years. Those who live with us know us best. Yet John says—after having seen Jesus in a variety of situations over a three-year period—that Jesus is *without* sin.

3:6 John appears to be saying here (and in vv. 8–10) that a Christian *cannot* sin. Yet in other passages in this letter, he points out that Christians can and do sin (e.g. 1:8,10; 2:1; 5:16). Some scholars feel that what John has in mind here is willful and deliberate sin (as against involuntary error). Other scholars stress the tense of the verb that John uses: a Christian does not *keep* on sinning. In other words, Christians do not habitually sin. Still other scholars feel that what John does here is to point out the ideal. This is what would happen if a Christian abided constantly in Christ.

3:10 John here spells out in clear, unequivocal terms the moral test, although he casts it in *negative* terms: a person "who does not do right is not a child of God."

UNIT 5—Love One Another / 1 John 3:11–24

Scripture

Love One Another

¹¹This is the message you heard from the beginning: We should love one another. ¹²Do not be like Cain, who belonged to the evil one and murdered his brother. And why did he murder him? Because his own actions were evil and his brother's were righteous. ¹³Do not be surprised, my brothers, if the world hates you. ¹⁴We know that we have passed from death to life, because we love our brothers. Anyone who does not love remains in death. ¹⁵Anyone who hates his brother is a murderer, and you know that no murderer has eternal life in him.

¹⁶This is how we know what love is: Jesus Christ laid down his life for us. And we ought to lay down our lives for our brothers. ¹⁷If anyone has material possessions and sees his brother in need but has no pity on him, how can the love of God be in him? ¹⁸Dear children, let us not love with words or tongue but with actions and in truth. ¹⁹This then is how we know that we belong to the truth, and how we set our hearts at rest in his presence ²⁰whenever our hearts condemn us. For God is greater than our hearts, and he knows everything.

²¹Dear friends, if our hearts do not condemn us, we have confidence before God ²²and receive from him anything we ask, because we obey his commands and do what pleases him. ²³And this is his command: to believe in the name of his Son, Jesus Christ, and to love one another as he commanded us. ²⁴Those who obey his commands live in him, and he in them. And this is how we know that he lives in us: We know it by the Spirit he gave us.

Group Questions

TO BEGIN / 15 Minutes (Choose 1 or 2)

❑ Who was your first "true love" growing up?
❑ What has been your most romantic moment?
❑ What one person has taught you a lot about Christian love? How?

READ SCRIPTURE AND DISCUSS / 30 Minutes

❑ What do you think Christians in the first century were encountering from the non-Christian world? From each other?
❑ What is the heart of John's message?
❑ Read, or recall, the story of Cain and Abel from Genesis 4:1–8. Why does John use the story in this passage? Where do you see "Cain-like" attitudes in yourself? Do you ever resemble the Peanuts character who said, "I love mankind; it's people I can't stand"?
❑ What is John's definition of love (vv. 16–18)? How does this definition differ from contemporary definitions of love? From some of your own previously held definitions? Who is the supreme example of love? Why?
❑ What are we assured of through loving others (vv. 14,19–20,24)?
❑ How would you like to consciously practice "Jesus-like" love this week? With your family? A friend? At church? In political or social issues? A difficult person? A person in need?
❑ How are answered prayers and obedience connected (vv. 18–22)? Will obedience affect what we pray for? How have you seen this to be true in your life? What area of your life do you need to examine regarding the link between obedience and the thing you are praying for?

TO CLOSE AND PRAY / 15–30 Minutes

❑ How did you receive Christ-like love during the past week? How will you need it in the coming week?
❑ How has this group shown the love of Christ to you?
❑ What prayer needs would you like to share?

Notes

3:11–24 In part one of this section (vv.11–18), John states the second test: true Christians love one another. Part two (vv. 19–24) is a parenthesis in which he comments on assurance and on obedience, both in the context of prayer.

3:11 *This is the message.* In 1:5 John used this phrase to introduce the great truth that God is light. Here he uses this phrase to introduce a second basic insight: love is at the center of the Christian life.

3:12 *Cain.* Cain was a farmer, the firstborn son of Adam and Eve. God was pleased with his brother Abel's offering, but not with his (Gen. 4:3-4). *belonged to the evil one.* The killing of one's brother is a specific example of the evil that Satan inspires (3:8). *why did he murder him?* Cain knew that unlike Abel's gift, his offering did not arise from the desire to do right. Therefore, because of his anger, Cain slew Abel (Gen. 4:6–7).

3:14 *from death to life.* The implication is that all people start out "dead." Satan is their father. They live in his realm. But by means of the rebirth process (2:29–3:2), it is possible to pass into the kingdom of life and become a child of God. *we know ... because we love.* Love is evidence that one possesses eternal life.

3:16–17 John offers a positive example of love: Jesus' sacrificial love for the human race. Cain's act sprang from hatred and *took* the life of another, while Jesus' act sprang from love and he gave his own life for others.

3:16 *This is how we know what love is.* Love is defined not by means of an intellectual proposition, but by a practical example. Jesus demonstrated love by giving his life for others.

3:17 While only a few Christians will be called upon to make the supreme sacrifice of their lives, *all* Christians can and must constantly share their possessions in order to relieve the material suffering that abounds in this world. *brother.* John asks his readers to consider the needs of a particular individual ("brother" is singular). "Loving everyone in general may be an excuse for loving nobody in particular" (Lewis). *pity.* Such self-giving love is not without emotion, even though it is primarily an action. John calls for genuine concern in the face of the plight of others. *how can the love of God be in him?* "As life does

not dwell in the murderer (v.15), love does not dwell in the miser" (Stott).

3:20 *whenever.* It is not an unusual experience for the conscience of a Christian to be troubled. *he knows everything.* The human conscience is not infallible, but God is. The implication is that God—who knows a person's innermost secrets—will be more merciful than the heart of that person.

3:22 Once again, John states a truth in a stark, unqualified way: if we ask, we will receive. Later, however (in 5:13), he will add the stipulation that people must ask "according to [God's] will." *obey.* Obedience is not the cause of answered prayer; it is the condition that motivates Christians to pray. Obedience is the evidence that they are moving in accordance with God's will, that they are in union with him, and that they will want to pray.

3:23–24 In these verses John shows the interconnection between obedience (the moral test), love (the social test), and belief (the doctrinal test), and how these relate to the question of union with God.

3:23 *to believe ... and to love.* John makes explicit what has previously been implicit: that at the core of Christianity there are two concerns—truth and love. In 1:5 he pointed out that the apostolic message is: God is *light.* In 3:11 he adds that the apostolic message is also: *love one another.* John clarifies that Christianity is not just a set of theological truths (though it is that). It is also a life of active self-giving to others. Neither belief nor love is sufficient without the other. These two themes will dominate the rest of his letter.

3:24 *those who obey his commands live in him.* Obedience and union are connected. Obedience to God's command to believe and love brings union with Christ. The outward, objective side of the Christian life (which is active love for others in obedience to the command of God) is connected to the inner, subjective experience of being in union with God. *he in them.* The Christian dwells in God; God dwells in the Christian. *how we know.* The Holy Spirit is the source of the believer's assurance that God does live in them (see 4:13).

UNIT 6—Test the Spirits / 1 John 4:1–6

Scripture

Test the Spirits

4 Dear friends, do not believe every spirit, but test the spirits to see whether they are from God, because many false prophets have gone out into the world. ²This is how you can recognize the Spirit of God: Every spirit that acknowledges that Jesus Christ has come in the flesh is from God, ³but every spirit that does not acknowledge Jesus is not from God. This is the spirit of the antichrist, which you have heard is coming and even now is already in the world.

⁴You, dear children, are from God and have overcome them, because the one who is in you is greater than the one who is in the world. ⁵They are from the world and therefore speak from the viewpoint of the world, and the world listens to them. ⁶We are from God, and whoever knows God listens to us; but whoever is not from God does not listen to us. This is how we recognize the Spiritᵃ of truth and the spirit of falsehood.

Group Questions

TO BEGIN / 15 Minutes (Choose 1 or 2)

❑ How did (do) you study for tests in school? Cram the night before? Pace yourself? Skim your notes? How did (do) you usually perform?

❑ What test can you remember causing you the most stress? A school exam? SAT? Driver's test? Performance test at work?

❑ How do you stay informed on current events? How confident are you of the accuracy of the sources you use?

READ SCRIPTURE AND DISCUSS / 30 Minutes

❑ What does John command in verse 1? Why? What else has he said about these false prophets (see 2:18–19)?

❑ How can a Christian distinguish a true prophet from a false one (see also 2:20–23)? What affirmation does the true prophet make?

❑ What do you believe about Jesus' nature? What difference does it make whether he was truly divine or not? Truly human or not?

❑ What "power" equips you to overcome, or stand against, false prophets? Why do people from Christian backgrounds get involved with cults? What helps you to find your way between being closed-minded to new theological insights, and being so open-minded that you lose your foundation?

CASE HISTORY: A college freshman returns from his first year at college with an obviously heightened awareness of spirituality. He has had contact with a number of Christian, Eastern and "New Age" groups and is attracted by the sincerity and depth of commitment he sees in each. However, he is bothered by how the Christians reject the others' teachings whereas the others absorb Christian teaching into their own. What do you say when he asks you what you think?

TO CLOSE AND PRAY / 15–30 Minutes

❑ How has this group helped you to work through some of your spiritual struggles or questions?

❑ How has God been moving in your life to help you know him better?

❑ What would you like this group to remember as they pray for you this week?

ᵃ6 Or *spirit*

Notes

4:1–6 In the final verse of the previous unit, John describes how Christians can know that God lives in them. They know this because the Holy Spirit bears inner witness to this fact (3:24). But the problem is that the secessionists make this same claim! They say that God's spirit speaks to them too. In fact, such private revelations are the source of their new doctrine. So, how can one distinguish between spirits? What is the difference between God's Spirit and false spirits? Is there an objective basis on which to accept or reject subjective claims? The answer relates to doctrine. That spirit which acknowledges that Jesus the Messiah came in the flesh is a spirit from God. Likewise, the opposite is true. Those spirits that do not acknowledge Jesus in this way are not from God (see also 2:20–23). Thus in this unit John expands on the doctrinal test—the third way by which to distinguish between true and false Christianity. There are two parts to this test. The first question is: to which spirit does one listen? Unless that spirit acknowledges Jesus as the Messiah come in the flesh, it is not of God (v. 2). The second question is: are you in submission to apostolic doctrine? Unless individuals acknowledge the truth of the Gospel (as taught from the beginning by apostles such as John), they are not following "the Spirit of truth" (v. 6).

4:1 *do not believe every spirit.* Having just claimed that Christians know God lives in them because the Holy Spirit bears witness to this fact, John hastens to qualify what he means. Not everything a spirit says is automatically of God. In fact, it is dangerous to accept uncritically everything that is said "in the name of God." Not everyone claiming inner revelation is hearing God's voice! *test.* The test by which to distinguish between spirits that John suggests is doctrinal in nature. It has to do with who Jesus is. False spirits will not acknowledge that Jesus of Nazareth (a fully human man) is the incarnate Christ (the divine Son of God). Notice that the focus of this test is upon the *spirit* who is the source of the prophecy—not upon what is said. In other words, true prophecy is not distinguished from false prophecy by the content of the prophecy itself. The question is: is the source of this prophecy divine or diabolical? (See also 1 Cor. 12:1–3; 14:29; 1 Thess. 5:19–22.) *spirits.* The issue is not whether supernatural spirits exist and actually inspire prophecy. This was assumed to be the case by almost everyone in the first century (see, for example, Mark 1:21–28,32–34). *prophets.* Prophets are those men and women who claim to speak on God's behalf. They allow the Holy Spirit—or another spirit—to speak through them. John does not deny the reality or the value of prophecy. He simply warns against false prophets, much as Jesus did (see Matt. 7:15; Mark 13:22–23).

4:2 To deny that Jesus, the Messiah, was truly human is incompatible with divine inspiration. Prophets who will not affirm this confession of faith are not of God. *acknowledges.* What John has in mind is not mere recognition of who Jesus is—since even the demons know him (Mark 1:24). Rather, what is called for is an open, positive, public declaration of faith in Jesus. *Jesus Christ has come in the flesh.* This is the second of three places in this epistle in which John touches upon how the secessionists view the person of Jesus. In 2:22–23, John says that they deny that Jesus is the Christ (i.e., that he is the Messiah). Here he asserts that they deny that Jesus, the Messiah, came in the flesh. In 5:6 (the third and final place where he deals with the question of Jesus' nature), John gets to the heart of the matter. What the secessionists are denying is that Jesus—as the Messiah—could have died.

4:4-6 John turns from his focus on prophets (true and false) to a consideration of those who follow each type of prophet. In verse 4 he directs his word to "you" (the Christians in Ephesus), in verse 5 he talks about "them" and "they" (the secessionists), while in verse 6 he talks about "we" (the apostles, of whom John is a representative).

4:4 *overcome.* The Christians to whom John writes have successfully resisted overtures by false prophets (the secessionists) to get them to believe new doctrines. They have not been deceived. *the one who is in you.* It is not by means of their own unaided strength that they are able to resist these false prophets. The source of their power is the Spirit of God who resides in them.

4:6 In contrast to the "world" (which stands in opposition to God, God's truth, and God's people), there is the church (which both believes God's truth and seeks to live it out). *recognize.* Those who respond positively to the apostolic preaching are those who are led by the Spirit of truth.

UNIT 7—God's Love and Ours / 1 John 4:7–21

Scripture

God's Love and Ours

*⁷Dear friends, let us love one another, for love comes from God. Everyone who loves has been born of God and knows God. ⁸Whoever does not love does not know God, because God is love. ⁹This is how God showed his love among us: He sent his one and only Son*ª *into the world that we might live through him. ¹⁰This is love: not that we loved God, but that he loved us and sent his Son as an atoning sacrifice for*ᵇ *our sins. ¹¹Dear friends, since God so loved us, we also ought to love one another. ¹²No one has ever seen God; but if we love one another, God lives in us and his love is made complete in us.*

¹³We know that we live in him and he in us, because he has given us of his Spirit. ¹⁴And we have seen and testify that the Father has sent his Son to be the Savior of the world. ¹⁵If anyone acknowledges that Jesus is the Son of God, God lives in him and he in God. ¹⁶And so we know and rely on the love God has for us.

God is love. Whoever lives in love lives in God, and God in him. ¹⁷In this way, love is made complete among us so that we will have confidence on the day of judgment, because in this world we are like him. ¹⁸There is no fear in love. But perfect love drives out fear, because fear has to do with punishment. The one who fears is not made perfect in love.

¹⁹We love because he first loved us. ²⁰If anyone says, "I love God," yet hates his brother, he is a liar. For anyone who does not love his brother, whom he has seen, cannot love God, whom he has not seen. ²¹And he has given us this command: Whoever loves God must also love his brother.

ª 9 Or *his only begotten Son*   ᵇ 10 Or *as the one who would turn aside his wrath, taking away*

Group Questions

TO BEGIN / 15 Minutes (Choose 1 or 2)

❏ What personality trait or strength did you get from your father? Your mother?
❏ What family event or experience stands out as an example of your family at their closest?
❏ How would you finish this sentence, "Love is like ..."?

READ SCRIPTURE AND DISCUSS / 30 Minutes

❏ Is the love discussed in this passage an action or a feeling? Why? What does this tell you about love?
❏ What is the source of human love? How can God's love be expressed through humans? In our motives? Our actions? Why is it a lie to say you love God but do not show that you love your "brother"?
❏ From verses 8–15, what do you learn about the relationship between the Father, Son and Spirit? About their relationship to us?
❏ How does the message that God's love drives out fear (v. 18) fit with the teaching that God is light (1:5)? In your life, when has "love" held too much fear? When has God's love cast out fear?
❏ If you want to do a better job of loving others, how should you go about it? What is the only way to improve (see vv. 15–16)?
❏ How do you want to love sacrificially this week? At home? At school? At work? In a difficult relationship? In how you plan your time? Your budget?

CASE HISTORY: Jim has tried, but he simply cannot get along with his 16-year-old son, Al. Jim is a task-oriented, success-minded driver. He is hard on himself. He is hard on his son. Al, by temperament, is just the opposite. His room is a disaster. His school work is never done on time, and he won't go out and get a job. Jim is at his wit's end. ADULTS: What advice would you give Jim? YOUTH: What advice would you give Al?

TO CLOSE AND PRAY / 15–30 Minutes

❏ Next week will be the last session in your study of 1 John. How has God spoken to you most clearly through this study and time together?
❏ What "serendipity" (unexpected blessing) have you received as a result of your time in this study?
❏ How would the group like to celebrate when the study is completed? A party? Dinner together?
❏ How has God moved in your life because of the prayers of others in this group? How can the group pray for you this week?

Notes

4:7 *love one another.* John will use this phrase three times in the next five verses (vv. 7,11,12). Each time, however, he uses it in a slightly different way. Here he urges his readers to love others because love originates in God. *everyone who loves.* Since "love comes from God," all acts of love are reflections of God's nature.

4:8 *whoever does not love does not know God.* To claim to be a Christian without living a life of love "is like claiming to be intimate with a foreigner whose language we cannot speak, or to have been born of parents whom we do not in any way resemble" (Stott). *God is love.* This is the second great assertion that John makes in this epistle about the nature of God. (His first assertion is that God is light.)

4:10 Love is initiated by God. Love is his posture toward the human race, and this love is given substance by the incarnation of his Son. It is not the other way around. People do not reach out to God with warm feelings or acts of devotion and thereby trigger his love for them. God is the primal lover. It is his action that draws out their response. Love begins with God. *an atoning sacrifice for our sins.* By this phrase John describes the saving work that Jesus did on behalf of the human race. The issue was sin. All had sinned. And sin had blocked fellowship with God. (A God who is light, by definition, can have no fellowship with darkness.) Human beings were unable to do anything to rectify their own situation. On the contrary, as sin did its corrupting work, they were drawn further and further away from God. Thus they needed help. They needed someone to take away their sin and so open up the way back to fellowship with God. This is what Jesus did. He came to earth as a man. He lived a perfect life. Because he had no sin of his own, it was possible for him to stand in the place of another and suffer the consequences of that person's sin. Because he was divine, it was possible for him to bear the sin of not just one other person but of all persons. So when Jesus died, it was not for his own sin, but for the sins of the world. He became "the atoning sacrifice for our sin." The idea of atonement is tied up with the Old Testament concept of substitution and sacrifice. In the Old Testament, sin was dealt with when a person symbolically placed his sins on an animal that he had brought to the temple. This animal had to be perfect—without spot or blemish. It was then sacrificed in place of the sinful (imperfect) person. Such substitutionary sacrifices were a picture of what Jesus would one day do once for all men and women.

4:11 *love one another.* This is the second time John uses this phrase. The basis for his exhortation this time is the demonstrated fact that "God so loved us." Jesus' sacrificial death on behalf of the human race assures people that God loves them, and thus releases in them the ability to love others. Because they are loved they can love.

4:12 *love one another.* In the third use of this phrase, John states that although God cannot be seen directly, his life can be experienced by people as they love one another. Since God is love, they know him when they love. *his love is made complete.* "When we love others, God's love for us has reached its full effect in creating the same kind of love as his in us" (Marshall).

4:13–16 John first elaborates on the phrase "God lives in us" (vv. 13–16), and then on the phrase "his love is made complete in us" (vv. 17-21)—both taken from verse 12.

4:18 *no fear in love.* The reason for the confidence believers will have on the day of judgment is that they know God to be their father in whose love they have dwelt. People cannot love and fear at the same moment; i.e., it is impossible to approach God with a heart filled both with servile fear and with an overflowing sense of his love for them and their love for him. The love casts out the fear. *fear has to do with punishment.* This is the root of the fear: they think God is going to punish them. They forget that they are his forgiven children.

4:19 The love believers exhibit is a response to the prior love of God for them. Love begets love.

4:20 Love for God is not merely warm, inner feelings. Love is not love unless it finds concrete expression via active caring for others. Furthermore, since it is far easier to love a visible person than to love the invisible God, to claim success in the harder task (loving God) while failing in the easier task (loving others) is an absurd and hopeless contradiction.

UNIT 8—Faith in the Son of God/Concluding Remarks / 1 John 5:1–21

Scripture

Faith in the Son of God

5 *Everyone who believes that Jesus is the Christ is born of God, and everyone who loves the father loves his child as well. [2]This is how we know that we love the children of God: by loving God and carrying out his commands. [3]This is love for God: to obey his commands. And his commands are not burdensome, [4]for everyone born of God overcomes the world. This is the victory that has overcome the world, even our faith. [5]Who is it that overcomes the world? Only he who believes that Jesus is the Son of God.*

[6]This is the one who came by water and blood—Jesus Christ. He did not come by water only, but by water and blood. And it is the Spirit who testifies, because the Spirit is the truth. [7]For there are three that testify: [8]the[a]Spirit, the water and the blood; and the three are in agreement. [9]We accept man's testimony, but God's testimony is greater because it is the testimony of God, which he has given about his Son. [10]Anyone who believes in the Son of God has this testimony in his heart. Anyone who does not believe God has made him out to be a liar, because he has not believed the testimony God has given about his Son. [11]And this is the testimony: God has given us eternal life, and this life is in his Son. [12]He who has the Son has life; he who does not have the Son of God does not have life.

Group Questions

TO BEGIN / 15 Minutes (Choose 1 or 2)

- ❏ In the Aesop's Fable, *The Tortoise and the Hare,* are you more like the steady, persistent tortoise, or the fast-starting, easily distracted hare? How so?
- ❏ Did you say a bedtime prayer as a child? What kind of prayer? Did Mom or Dad join you?

READ SCRIPTURE AND DISCUSS / 30 Minutes

- ❏ What kind of love comes along with our new birth (vv. 1–3)? Why are God's commands not a burden? Is obedience ever a burden for you? Is there a difference between something being difficult and being a burden?
- ❏ How are you doing at loving God? Using the "love test" from verses 1–3, how are you doing at loving others? How does your obedience to God affect your love for others?
- ❏ What is the power source for overcoming the world? How have you seen faith (belief), love and obedience (vv. 1–3) to be interconnected in your life? What lie is John combating (remember the group who had split off from the church)?
- ❏ What are the three witnesses to Jesus Christ (v. 7)? What do water and blood refer to (see Note 5:6)? What happened at Jesus' baptism (Mark 1:9–11)? Why is it important to emphasize Jesus' death and resurrection? How does the Spirit testify to Jesus?
- ❏ What has convinced you that true life is found in Jesus? What further "proof" do you need?
- ❏ What is the condition for prayer to be answered (vv. 14–15)? What does it mean to pray in Jesus' name? How often are you prompted to pray for someone you see struggling with sin in their life?
- ❏ What might be the sin that leads to death (see Mark 3:22–30)? Why do the very fears of those who worry about having committed this sin prove that they have not done so?

[Scripture and questions continued on page 28]

[a]7,8 Late manuscripts of the Vulgate *testify in heaven: the Father, the Word and the Holy Spirit, and these three are one.*
[8]*And there are three that testify on earth: the* (not found in any Greek manuscript before the sixteenth century)

Notes

5:1–4a Here John ties together the three tests of faith. "The real link between the three tests is seen to be the new birth. Faith, love and obedience are the natural growth which follows a birth from above" (Stott).

5:1 believes. The tense of the verb indicates that belief is here seen as the *result* of new birth, not its cause. Belief on the part of Christians is clear proof that they have been born of God. Elsewhere, John points to faith as the *condition* of the new birth. The two emphases are complementary: faith enables the new birth to happen, and faith is the sign that it has taken place.

5:2 John states another complementary truth. In 4:20–21, he pointed out that in order to love God, one must also love his children. Here he points out that one loves the children of God by loving the Father. **carrying out his commands.** Love for God involves moral obedience. Love and obedience are inexorably linked (John 15:10–12).

5:3 burdensome. Obedience to the thousands of often picayune rules and regulations promulgated by the scribes and Pharisees was indeed a heavy burden. But obedience to God does not exasperate the Christian, since God's laws are of quite a different character (e.g., they are life-giving), and the faith of Christians provides the power for obedience.

5:4–12 John has one last statement to make before he concludes his letter. The crucial issue in this whole matter of orthodoxy versus apostasy hinges on one's view of Jesus. If faith is rightly directed at the historic Jesus, then (by implication) correct lifestyle and loving relationships will flow from that commitment. But if not—if the Jesus who is honored is more a product of fancy than fact—then quite a different world view will flourish (as the secessionists demonstrate). So John ends where he began—with his testimony to Jesus.

5:4b our faith. This is the source of the overcoming power of the Christian—confidence and trust that Jesus is the Son of God (see 5:5).

5:6-9 How is it that one comes to faith in Jesus? By means of reliable witnesses, John answers. He names three such witnesses: the water, the blood, and the Holy Spirit.

5:6 by water and blood. By these two phrases, John is referring to Jesus' baptism and death. These events are crucial in understanding who Jesus is. At his baptism, Jesus publicly identified himself with the sins of the people (even though he himself was without sin). At his death, Jesus died to take away those sins. Water and blood would also remind John's readers of the ordinances of baptism and communion. **not ... by water alone.** Both the baptism and the crucifixion are crucial in understanding Jesus. **it is the Spirit who testifies.** John has already stated the fact that there is an inner witness given by the Holy Spirit as to the truth of who Jesus is (see 3:24; 4:13; 1 Cor. 12:3). **the Spirit is the truth.** The Holy Spirit is the third witness, and is qualified to be such because the Spirit is, in inner essence, truth itself.

5:9 John clarifies the authority behind these three witnesses. It is God himself. He makes explicit the object of the three-fold witness. It is Jesus his Son. **greater.** In a law court, testimony is accepted when it is corroborated by two or three witnesses (Deut. 19:15). How much more substantial is the three-fold testimony of God!

5:10 The purpose of this testimony is to produce faith. To accept the testimony is synonymous with believing in Jesus. **believes in.** It is one thing to *believe* Jesus. It is another to *believe in* Jesus. To believe Jesus is to accept what he says as true. To believe in Jesus is to accept who he is. It is to trust him completely and commit one's life to him. **a liar.** To reject this triple testimony is to disbelieve God (who is the essence of truth). It is to attribute falsehood to God (see 1:10).

5:11 eternal life. In receiving the testimony and thus receiving the Son, one also receives eternal life. The Greek word which is here translated "eternal" means "that which belongs to the coming age." But since that age has already broken into the present age, eternal life can be enjoyed even now.

5:14 assurance. By this word John refers to the bold confidence Christians have—that they can approach God in prayer and freely speak their minds. **according to his will.** In 3:22, John says that the condition for answered prayer is obedient behavior. Here John adds another condition: what we ask must be in accord with God's plans and purposes (see also Matt. 26:39,42).

[Notes continued on page 29]

Scripture (Continued)

Concluding Remarks

¹³*I write these things to you who believe in the name of the Son of God so that you may know that you have eternal life. ¹⁴This is the confidence we have in approaching God: that if we ask anything according to his will, he hears us. ¹⁵And if we know that he hears us—whatever we ask—we know that we have what we asked of him.*

¹⁶*If anyone sees his brother commit a sin that does not lead to death, he should pray and God will give him life. I refer to those whose sin does not lead to death. There is a sin that leads to death. I am not saying that he should pray about that. ¹⁷All wrongdoing is sin, and there is sin that does not lead to death.*

¹⁸*We know that anyone born of God does not continue to sin; the one who was born of God keeps him safe, and the evil one cannot harm him. ¹⁹We know that we are children of God, and that the whole world is under the control of the evil one. ²⁰We know also that the Son of God has come and has given us understanding, so that we may know him who is true. And we are in him who is true—even in his Son Jesus Christ. He is the true God and eternal life.*

²¹*Dear children, keep yourselves from idols.*

Group Questions (Continued)

❏ If 1 John were dropped from the Bible, what would be missing from the story of God's redemptive work in history?

CASE HISTORY: Your two closest friends are not Christian. One says that he was a Christian once, but he would "rather have his fun." The other openly ridicules the Christian faith as a "bunch of myths." How should you pray for these friends?

TO CLOSE AND PRAY / 15–30 Minutes

❏ As you reflect back on your time with this group, how has your experience impacted you in the greatest way?
❏ How have you appreciated each individual in the group? Focus on one person at a time and give everyone a chance to share what they've appreciated about this person.
❏ Would you like the group to continue? If so, what would need to change? What should stay the same? (See also page 4.)
❏ How would you like this group to continue praying for you?

5:15 *he hears us.* By this phrase John means "he hears us favorably." To know that God hears is to know that "we have what we asked." ***we have what we asked.*** "Our petitions are granted at once: the results of the granting are perceived in the future" (Plummer).

5:16 John now offers a specific illustration of how prayer operates. ***brothers.*** John is probably not using this term to refer to other Christians, but rather in the broader sense of "neighbors," as is evident from how he writes about these people. ***a sin that leads to death.*** Although John's readers probably understood what he was referring to, it is not at all clear now what this phrase means. A specific kind of sin is probably not in view here, but rather a lifestyle of habitual, willing, and persistent sinning. ***I am not saying that he should pray about that.*** While John does not forbid prayer for those involved in a "sin that leads to death," he does not advise it, since he doubts its value in such a case.

5:18 The first affirmation relates to Christian behavior. "It expresses the truth, not that he cannot ever slip into acts of sin, but rather that he does not persist in it habitually ... The new birth results in new behavior. Sin and the child of God are incompatible. They may occasionally meet; they cannot live together in harmony" (Stott).

5:19 The second affirmation is that they are, indeed, "children of God." They are part of the family of God and in relationship with the other children of God.

5:20 The third affirmation is that they really do know what is true (over against the secessionists who are promoting a new truth). ***has come and has given us understanding.*** By this phrase John highlights the two-fold work of Christ. He came, and thus provided salvation. But he also brought new understanding of the nature of God. Both redemption and revelation are central to the ministry of Jesus. ***understanding.*** The power or ability to know what is actually so. Specifically, Jesus gave Christians the power to perceive the true God over against false idols (see v. 21).

ACKNOWLEDGEMENTS

In preparing notes such as these, there is a strong dependence upon the tools of New Testament research (e.g. Arndt and Gingrich Greek-English Lexicon; Bible Dictionaries; New Testament Introductions; etc.). In addition, use has been made of various commentaries. While it is not possible as one would desire, given the scope and aim of this book, to acknowledge in detail the input of each author, the source of direct quotes and special insights is given. The three key commentaries that were used are: Raymond E. Brown, *The Epistles of John* (The Anchor Bible), Garden City, NY: Doubleday and Company, Inc., 1982; I. Howard Marshall, *The Epistles of John* (The New International Commentary on the New Testament), Grand Rapids: Wm. B. Eerdmans Publishing Co., 1978; and John R. W. Stott, *The Epistles of John* (Tyndale New Testament Commentaries), London: The Tyndale Press, 1964.

In addition, reference was made to William Barclay, *The Letters of John and Jude* (The Daily Study Bible), Edinburgh: The Saint Andrew Press, 1958; F. F. Bruce, *The Epistle of John*, Grand Rapids: Wm. B. Eerdmans Publishing Co., 1970; C. H. Dodd, *The Johannine Epistles* (MNTC), London: Hodder and Stoughton, 1946; Hass, deJonge, Swellongrebel, *A Translator's Handbook on the Letters of John*, London: United Bible Societies, 1972; J. L. Houlden, *A Commentary on the Johannine Epistles* (Harper's New Testament Commentaries), New York: Harper & Row, 1973; Marilyn Kunz and Catherine Schell, *1 John and James* (Neighborhood Bible Studies), Wheaton: Tyndale House Publishers, 1965; and Rodney A. Whitacre, *Johannine Polemic: The Role of Tradition and Theology* (SBL Dissertation Series 67), Chico, CA: Scholars Press, 1982.

Thanks to A.D. Cox who provided insights into The Church of the Living Word (The Walk). A word is in order about the definition of the word "cult" as used in this manuscript. The term is not meant in the pejorative sense. Rather, it is used to denote those groups who have departed from historic Christianity as defined by 1 John. Furthermore, as will become clear from the text, there is no intention to create an "us/them" mentality when it comes to cults. It is our hope, however, to define clearly the differences that do exist between Christianity and cults.

TIME
FOR A
CHECK-UP

SEVEN COMMON SMALL GROUP AILMENTS
AND HOW TO OVERCOME THEM

ARE YOU FEELING A LITTLE
NERVOUS ABOUT BEING IN A SMALL GROUP?

SYMPTOMS: Do you break out into a sweat at the mention of small groups. Does your mouth turn to sawdust when it comes "your turn" to share? To pray?

PRESCRIPTION: Take this test to see if you are ready to belong to a small group. If you answer "yes" on seven out of ten questions below, you are probably ready to take the plunge.

1. Are you looking for a place where you can deal with the serious questions in your life right now?   ☐ Yes   ☐ No

2. Are you open to the possibility that God has something special for your life?
   ☐ Yes   ☐ No

3. Are you open to the Bible as the source where God's will for your life can be explored?
   ☐ Yes   ☐ No

4. Are you able to admit that you do not have all the answers about the Bible? God? Your own life?   ☐ Yes   ☐ No

5. Are you able to let others have questions about the Bible or God?   ☐ Yes   ☐ No

6. Are you willing to accept people in the group that are "Prodigal Sons" and have a long way to go in their spiritual faith?   ☐ Yes   ☐ No

7. Are you willing to keep anything that is shared in this group in strict confidence?   ☐ Yes   ☐ No

8. Are you willing to share in the responsibility for the group and to support group members with your prayers?   ☐ Yes   ☐ No

9. Are you willing to give priority to this group for a short period of time (such as six to twelve weeks) and consider making a longer commitment after this time?
   ☐ Yes   ☐ No

10. Are you excited about the possibilities of belonging to a group that could make a difference in your life?   ☐ Yes   ☐ No

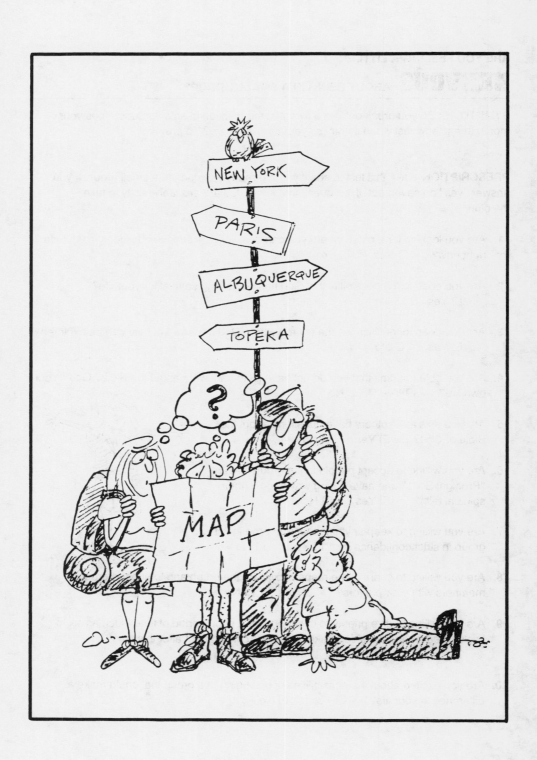

ARE YOU FEELING A LITTLE
CONFUSED ABOUT YOUR PURPOSE?

SYMPTOMS: Do you feel like you are playing on a team that doesn't have any rules? Any direction? Any idea of what you want to do or accomplish? Or where you are going?

PRESCRIPTION: Before you ever started the group, you should have decided on a COVENANT that spelled out your purpose, rules, expectations, etc. If you didn't, call "time out" and decide *together* on a covenant.

Here's how. Take the first sentence below and ask everyone to finish the sentence. Then, try to come up with a one sentence statement that you all can agree to. "The purpose of our group is . . ."

Then, take the second sentence and decide on your specific goals, etc. . . . until you have decided on your GROUP COVENANT. This becomes your game plan.

1. The purpose of our group is . . .

2. Our specific goals are . . .

3. We will meet _____ times, every _____ week, after which we will evaluate our group.

4. We will meet: Day of week _____ from _____ (time) to _____ .

5. We will meet at _____ , or rotate the place where we meet.

6. In addition to the study of the Bible, we will . . .

7. We will adhere to the following ground rules:
- ☐ The leader of the group will be . . . or we will rotate the leadership.
- ☐ The host for each meeting (other than the leader) will be . . . or we will rotate this responsibility.
- ☐ Food/refreshments will be . . .
- ☐ Baby-sitting, etc.

8. In addition to these general rules, we will agree to the following disciplines:
- ☐ Attendance: To give priority to the group meetings
- ☐ Participation: To share responsibility for the group
- ☐ Confidentiality: To keep anything that is said strictly confidential
- ☐ Accountability: To give permission to group members to hold you accountable for goals you set for yourself
- ☐ Accessibility: To give one another the right to call upon you for help in time of need—even in the middle of the night.

ARE YOU FEELING A LITTLE

DISTANT FROM THE OTHERS IN YOUR GROUP?

SYMPTOMS: Does your group start off like a Model A Ford on a cold morning? Or sag in the middle when you get to the Bible study? Do you find some of the people do all the talking . . . and others never get out of their "shell"?

PRESCRIPTION: Use the "flow questions" in the margin, next to the Scripture text, to guide the discussion. The questions are carefully designed to explode like time bombs on three levels of sharing: (1) TO BEGIN—to break the ice, (2) READ SCRIPTURE AND DISCUSS—to discuss the Scripture text, and (3) TO CLOSE AND PRAY—to take inventory of your own life.

1 **TO BEGIN / 10–15 Minutes:** Start off with a few good "stories" about your childhood or human-interest experiences. The better the "stories" at this level . . . the deeper the group will share at the close. (There is a close parallel between "childlikeness" and "Christlikeness".)

> **TO BEGIN / 15 Minutes** (Choose 1 or 2)
> ❑ What mail will you open first: Bills? Official looking stuff? Personal mail? Love letter?
> ❑ When you care for someone, are you more likely to send a funny card or a touching one?

2 **READ SCRIPTURE AND DISCUSS / 30–45 Minutes:** You read the Scripture text at this point and go around on the first question. The questions are designed both to get you into the text and to help you reflect on the Scripture's meaning for your own life. The questions will help to draw your group together in a way that all can participate and share. By the way, you do not have to finish all the questions. Save time for the TO CLOSE AND PRAY section.

> **READ SCRIPTURE AND DISCUSS / 30 Minutes**
> ❑ Where is Paul writing from? Why? Who is he writing to? (Hint: Go back and read the Introduction, especially the paragraph on Origin and Occasion.)
> ❑ Who was the Apostle Paul in your spiritual life—who introduced you to Jesus Christ and cared about your spiritual growth?

3 **TO CLOSE AND PRAY / 15–30 Minutes** This is the heart of the Bible study. The purpose is to take inventory of your own life and share with the group "what God is telling you to do." The questions are "high risk"; that is, the group is asked to share on a "need level," before moving on to prayer.

> **TO CLOSE AND PRAY / 15-30 Minutes**
> ❑ If you had a spiritual check-up today, what would the doctor prescribe?
> ❑ How can this Bible study group help you reach your spiritual goals?
> ❑ Who is someone you would like to invite to this group next week?
> ❑ What would you like this group to remember in prayer for you this week?

Scripture

Thanksgiving and Prayer

³I thank my God every time I remember you. ⁴In all my prayers for all of you, I always pray with joy ⁵because of your partnership in the gospel from the first day until now, ⁶being confident of this, that he who began a good work in you will carry it on to completion until the day of Christ Jesus. ⁷It is right for me to feel this way about all of you, since I have you in my heart;

Group Questions

TO BEGIN: What mail will you open first:Bills? Official looking stuff? Personal mail? Love letter?

READ SCRIPTURE AND DISCUSS: Where is Paul writing from? Why? Who is he writing to? (Hint: Go back and read the Introduction, especially the paragraph on Origin and Occasion).

TO CLOSE AND PRAY: If you had a spiritual check-up today, what would the doctor prescribe?

ARE YOU FEELING A LITTLE
INTIMIDATED BY THE BIBLE SCHOLARS IN YOUR GROUP?

SYMPTOMS: Are you afraid that your ignorance about the Bible could be embarrassing? For instance: if someone asked you who Melchizedek was, what would you say? If you said "an old linebacker for the Raiders", you would be wrong. Twice wrong.

PRESCRIPTION: Don't despair. Most of the people in your group don't know either. And that's O.K. This Bible study group is for BEGINNERS. And for BEGINNERS, there are Notes on the opposite page to help you keep up to speed with the rest of the group.

NOTES include:

- ☐ Definitions of significant words.

- ☐ Historical background: the political, social, economic context behind the words in the text.

- ☐ Geographical setting: facts about the country, terrain, lakes, crops, roads, and religious shrines.

- ☐ Cultural perspective: lifestyles, homes, customs, holidays, traditions, and social patterns.

- ☐ Archeological evidence: recent findings that sheds light on the Bible events.

- ☐ Summary/Commentary: recap of the argument to keep the passage in the context of the whole book.

Notes

1:3 *every time I remember you*. This is a difficult phrase to translate from the Greek. What it seems to mean is that during his times of prayer, Paul "was compelled by love to mention his Philippian friends. This means, then, that Paul gave thanks not whenever he happened to remember them, but that he regularly gave thanks for them and mentioned them to God at set times of prayer" (Hawthorne).

1:4 *with joy*. "Joy" is a theme that pervades Philippians. This is the first of some fourteen times that Paul will use the word in this epistle. He mentions "joy" more often in this short epistle

***confirming the gospel*.** These are legal terms. The reference is to Paul's defense before the Roman court, in which he hopes to be able not only to vindicate himself and the gospel from false charges, but to proclaim the gospel in life-changing power to those in the courtroom. (See Ac 26 for an example of how Paul did this when he stood in court before Agrippa and Festus.)

1:8 *I long*. Yet another word characteristic of Paul. He uses it seven of the nine times it is found in the New Testament. This is a strong word and expresses the depth of Paul's feelings for them, his desire to be with them, and the wish to minister

ARE YOU FEELING A LITTLE

TEMPTED TO KEEP THE GROUP JUST FOR YOURSELF?

SYMPTOMS: Two feelings surface: (1) if we let anyone into our group, it would destroy our "closeness", and/or (2) if we let anyone into our group, we would not have time enough to share.

PRESCRIPTION: Study the ministry of Jesus and the early church: the need for "closeness" and the danger of "closedness." How did Jesus respond to his own disciples when they asked to "stay together" and build a "monument." Note the Story of the Transfiguration in Mark 9:2–13.

SOLUTION #1: Pull up an empty chair during the prayer time at the close of the group and pray that God will "fill the chair" with someone by the next week.

SOLUTION #2: When the group reaches seven or eight in number, divide into two groups of 4—4 at the dining table, 4 at the kitchen table—when the time comes for the Bible study . . . and reshuffle the foursomes every week so that you keep the whole group intact, but sub-group for the discussion time.

THREE PART AGENDA FOR GROUP USING THE SUB-GROUP MODEL

GATHERING/15 Minutes/All Together.
Refreshments are served as the group gathers and assignments are made to sub-groups of 4.

SHARING/30–45 Minutes/Groups of 4.
Sub-groups are formed to discuss the questions in the margin of the text.

CARING/15–30 Minutes/All Together.
Regather the whole group to share prayer requests and pray.

ARE YOU FEELING A LITTLE

BORED WITH YOUR BIBLE STUDY GROUP?

SYMPTOMS: You feel "tired" before the meeting starts. And worse after it is over. The sharing is mostly a "head-trip". One person is absent three weeks in a row. Another is chronically late. You feel like your time could be better spent doing something else, but you don't know how to say it.

PRESCRIPTION: You may be having a group "mid-life" crisis. Here are three suggestions.

1. Call "time out" for a session and evaluate your Covenant (page 5). Are you focused on your "purpose"? Your goals? Are you sticking to your rules? Should you throw out some of your rules? (Nobody said you can't.)

2. Check to see if your group is hitting on all three cylinders for a healthy small group. (1) Nurture/Bible Study, (2) Support for one another, and (3) Mission/Task. Here's a way to test yourself.
   On a scale from 1 to 10, circle a number to indicate how you feel your group is doing on each of these three cylinders.

ON NURTURE/BIBLE STUDY: Getting to know the Bible. Letting God speak to you about His plans for your life through the Scripture.

We're doing a LOUSY JOB	1	2	3	4	5	6	7	8	9	10	We're doing a GREAT JOB

ON SUPPORT: Getting to know each other. Caring about each other. Holding each other accountable for the best God has for you.

We're doing a LOUSY JOB	1	2	3	4	5	6	7	8	9	10	We're doing a GREAT JOB

ON MISSION/TASK: Reaching out to others in need. Drawing people into the group, or sponsoring another group.

We're doing a LOUSY JOB	1	2	3	4	5	6	7	8	9	10	We're doing a GREAT JOB

3. Consider the possibility that God is saying it is time to shut down the group. Take time for a party. Give everyone a chance to share what the group has meant to him/her and what he/she will remember most about the group.

ARE YOU FEELING A LITTLE

ITCHY ABOUT DOING SOMETHING MORE?

SYMPTOMS: You're feeling tired of just sitting around studying the Bible. You have friends who are really hurting. Struggling. God seems to be saying something, but you don't know just what.

PRESCRIPTION: Consider the possibility that God is asking your group to split up and give birth to some new groups. Here are some steps:

1. Brainstorm together. Go around and have everyone finish the first sentence below. Then, go around on the second sentence, etc.

   I am concerned about a group for . . . (such as . . . "a group for young mothers, single parents, blended families, parents of adolescents, men at my office, young couples, empty nesters . . ." etc.).

   I wish we could . . .

   I would be willing to . . .

2. Make a list of prospects (people from the fringe of the church or outside of any church) that you would like to invite to a dinner party at which you could explain "what this Bible study group has meant to you."

3. Write each of these people a hand-written invitation on your personal stationary, inviting them to the dinner party at your home. (Don't bother to use the church bulletin. Nobody reads that.)

HOW TO TURN YOUR GROUP INTO A MISSIONARY GROUP

ORIGINAL
STUDY
GROUP

Holds a dinner party
for their friends
and prospects

NEW STUDY GROUPS ARE FORMED/ORIGINAL GROUP THE LEADERS

(P.S. You can still get back together with the whole group once a month for a "reunion" to share exciting "stories" of your new groups.

GALATIANS

Introduction to
GALATIANS

Audience

Paul tells us he is writing "to the churches in Galatia" (1:2). But where are these churches located? This is a problem, because in 25 B.C. the Romans created a new imperial province that they named Galatia. This new province was made up of the original kingdom of Galatia plus a new region to the south, forged out of territory originally belonging to six other regions. So when a first-century writer speaks of Galatia, it is not always clear whether he is referring to the original territory in the north, or the new province extending southward. In these notes, though scholarly opinion is divided at this point, the view is taken that Paul was writing to the churches he planted in South Galatia (Pisidian Antioch, Iconium, Lystra, and Derbe) during his first missionary journey described in Acts 13-14.

Date

The date of Paul's epistle depends on whether he was writing to churches in North or South Galatia. If Paul had been writing to congregations in North Galatia, the letter could not have been written before his third missionary expedition (after the journey mentioned in Acts 16:6 and 18:23, around A.D. 55). On the other hand, if Paul were writing to the churches in the southern region, as we are assuming, the epistle to the Galatians is his earliest letter (written in A.D. 48 or 49), possibly while he was in Syrian Antioch just prior to the Council in Jerusalem (Acts 15:6–21).

Theme

The Issue

Paul was furious and he didn't care who knew it. "You foolish Galatians!" he cried, "who has bewitched you?" (3:1). He felt so strongly because the issue he was addressing in this letter was not a minor matter of church policy. It struck right to the heart of the Gospel.

Apparently some legalistic Jewish-Christians (Judaizers) had been stirring up trouble. They had twisted the Gospel into something Jesus never intended, and then they had cast aspersions on Paul. "Who is that fellow, anyway? He wasn't one of the Twelve. He is a self-appointed apostle. No wonder he left out some crucial parts of the message. Let us set you straight. ..." And the Galatians were taken in, so it seems. Paul wrote, "I am astonished that you are so quickly deserting the one who called you by the grace of Christ and are turning to a different Gospel" (1:6).

What were the Judaizers saying? At first glance, they seemed to be adding only a little to the message. "Believe in Christ," they were saying (they were Christians), "but also be circumcised" (6:12). Now to be circumcised was not such a high requirement, but Paul saw the implications. If the Galatians let themselves be circumcised, it would be but the first step back to keeping the whole Law (5:3). This is slavery (4:9). This is bondage (5:1). This is not the Gospel. The Gospel is that salvation is a free gift, by grace. If you add anything else to grace, salvation is no longer free. It then becomes a matter of doing the "other thing."

The core issue in Galatians is justification. How does a person gain right standing before God? The Judaizers said that Christ (grace) plus circumcision (law-keeping) equals right standing. Paul's equation was different: Christ (grace) plus *nothing else* equals right standing. Works are excluded from Paul's equation. "Know that a man is not justified by observing the law, but by faith in Jesus Christ. So we, too, have put our faith in Christ Jesus that we may be justified by faith in Christ and not by observing the law, because by observing the law no one will be justified" (2:16). This key verse sums up Paul's argument.

The Implications

To the modern reader, it may seem at times as if Paul is getting worked up over a relatively small issue. After all, the important thing is to believe in Jesus, and all the parties agreed to that. But in fact, as history demonstrated, this issue was profound. Paul's concerns were more than validated. The underlying issue related to the universality of Christianity. Was Christianity for all people in all cultures (as Paul was arguing), or was it only a Jewish sect? To be a Christian, did you first have to become a Jew (which is the implication of the Judaizers' argument)? Did you have to accept Jewish customs, live a Jewish lifestyle, and submit to Jewish laws? If so (if the Judaizers had won), Christianity would probably have died out in the first century.

As we know, Christianity did not disappear along with all the Palestinian sects. Rather, the church was able to expand into the Graeco-Roman world because the Gospel was truly universal. It was not tied to temple sacrifice and the Law of Moses, about which most pagans neither knew nor cared. The Judaizers wanted a Christianity circumscribed by Jewish exclusiveness, taboos, and customs—in which, by force, Gentile believers would always be second-class citizens. Paul fought this with vehemence and passion, as had other believers from Stephen onward; so Christianity became the transcultural world religion Christ intended (Matt. 28:19–20).

The Relationship between Galatians and Romans

It is obvious that there is a close thematic connection between Galatians and Romans. Galatians appears to be Paul's first attempt at wrestling with the issue of justification by faith alone. Paul does so in the context of having to deal with a local problem. Romans, on the other hand, is a more studied consideration of the same issue. It is an eloquent, carefully stated, logical argument, which stands as one of the finest pieces of theological writing ever penned. Paul lifts the core of his argument from Galatians and shapes and refines it into a theological whole in Romans. As J.B. Lightfoot wrote: "The Epistle to the Galatians stands in relation to the Roman letter, as the rough model to the finished statue" (*St. Paul's Epistle to the Galatians*, p. 49).

Structure

After a terse greeting (1:1–5) and pronouncement of anathema against the troublemakers (1:6–10), Paul launches into his first major theme: his *personal defense*, in which he deals with the charge that he is not a real apostle (1:11–2:21). This is followed by a *doctrinal defense*, in which he shows that Christianity lived under the Law is inferior to Christianity lived by faith (3:1–4:31). On the basis of these two arguments, he then shows what true Christian freedom is (5:1–6:10), ending with an unusual conclusion written in his own hand (6:11–18).

UNIT 1—Salutation / Galatians 1:1–5

Scripture

1 *Paul, an apostle—sent not from men nor by man, but by Jesus Christ and God the Father, who raised him from the dead—²and all the brothers with me,*

To the churches in Galatia:

³Grace and peace to you from God our Father and the Lord Jesus Christ, ⁴who gave himself for our sins to rescue us from the present evil age, according to the will of our God and Father, ⁵to whom be glory for ever and ever. Amen.

Group Questions

Every group meeting has three goals: **(1) To Begin** (15 Minutes) to break the ice; **(2) Read Scripture and Discuss** (30 Minutes); and **(3) To Close and Pray** (15–30 Minutes). Try to keep on schedule. The most important time is the prayer time.

TO BEGIN / 15 Minutes (Choose 1 or 2)

❏ When you were junior high age, where did you go for some peace and quiet?
❏ What is the closest you have come to needing to be rescued? What happened?
❏ How long are the letters you write: Short and sweet? Until writer's cramp sets in? What letters?!

READ SCRIPTURE AND DISCUSS / 30 Minutes

❏ What, according to Paul's claim in verse 1, gives him the right to be heard?
❏ PAST: What did Jesus Christ voluntarily do for Paul and the Galatians ... and us (v. 4)?
❏ At what point in your life were you most aware of your need to be changed by Jesus Christ? What happened?
❏ PRESENT: What ongoing spiritual blessings are available now (v. 3)?
❏ What blessing or gift from God is most needed in your life right now?
❏ FUTURE: What will God deservedly receive for the rest of time (v. 5)?
❏ What spiritual commitment or goal do you feel God calling you to make for his honor and glory?
❏ How can this group help you reach your spiritual goals?

TO CLOSE AND PRAY / 15–30 Minutes

❏ What motivated you to come to this Bible study?
❏ What would you like to see happen in this group? What are your expectations?
❏ Have you agreed on a group "contract" (see p. 4)?
❏ Who would you like to invite to the next meeting?
❏ How would you like this group to remember you in prayer this week?

Notes

1:1–5 This greeting is chilly in tone by comparison to other greetings sent to churches which Paul founded. He says nothing in praise of the Galatians' activities and, in fact, is quite defensive (since apparently they are questioning his authority as an apostle).

1:1 *Paul.* While some scholars dispute whether or not Paul actually wrote all the epistles traditionally assigned to him, virtually everyone accepts that he was the author of Galatians. In fact, Galatians is often used as the model by which to test the "genuineness" of other epistles. *apostle.* This NT word means "a special messenger," and was used at first to denote the Twelve who were originally chosen by Jesus. Very soon, however, the term became more inclusive, being applied first to Matthias who replaced Judas Iscariot (Acts 1:26) and then to others (Rom. 16:7; 1 Cor. 15:7–9) including Paul. The apostles were those individuals who were regarded as final authorities in matters of faith and practice. *not from men ... but by Jesus.* Paul emphasizes that his apostleship derives not from any human intermediary (as does, for example, the authority of the men in 2 Cor. 8:23 Paul calls "apostles of the church"—which is the literal translation of the verse). Rather his commission was received directly from the resurrected Christ on the Damascus road. This is important because apparently his opponents were giving out a different story in their attempt to demean his authority. The authority of a person is directly related to the authority of the one who does the commissioning. Hence when Paul speaks, he does so with Christ's authority.

1:2 *to the churches.* This was a circular letter sent primarily to the churches in Pisidian Antioch, Iconian, Lystra, and Derbe (Acts 13:14–14:23), though other congregations may have sprung up in the area by the time of its composition. *Galatia.* The Roman province of Galatia was located in what is now the central part of Turkey (see a Bible map). The original kingdom of Galatia in the north had been settled by Celtic tribespeople who had migrated from the Danube basin in Central Europe to Asia Minor. (The Celts also migrated into Gaul and Britain.)

1:3 *grace and peace.* These words are typically used by Paul to begin a letter, pointing to God's goodwill towards humanity expressed in the saving work of Christ (grace), and to the resultant quality of life with God that ensues for those who have opened themselves to the operation of this divine grace (peace).

1:4 "This is probably the earliest written statement in the NT about the significance of the death of Christ" (F. F. Bruce). *gave himself.* The idea is of voluntary sacrifice for a specific purpose. *for our sins.* A crucial phrase, indicating that this was not just the death of a martyr, but was rather an act of cosmic significance which made possible the forgiveness of sin (and hence opened the way for men and women back to God). Such a statement defining the purpose of Christ's death is often found in primitive summaries of the Gospel (1 Cor. 15:3). *rescue.* To be rescued from bondage is a key idea in the epistle. The word carries the idea of being delivered from the power of another, and is used elsewhere in the NT to describe the rescue of the Israelites from Egypt (Acts 7:34) and the release of Peter from prison and from Herod (Acts 12:11). Here it is used metaphorically to describe salvation by pointing to Christ's triumph over the bondage of evil. *the present evil age.* There are two ages: "this age" which is evil and under Satan's control, and "the age to come" which was inaugurated when Christ came. Both ages run side by side at the moment. In becoming a Christian, a person is shifted, as it were, from one mode of reality into the other—escaping from the track that leads to ultimate death to that which gives eternal life.

1:5 *to whom be glory.* A doxology in praise of God's deliverance.

37

UNIT 2—No Other Gospel / Galatians 1:6-10

Scripture

No Other Gospel

⁶*I am astonished that you are so quickly deserting the one who called you by the grace of Christ and are turning to a different gospel—*⁷*which is really no gospel at all. Evidently some people are throwing you into confusion and are trying to pervert the gospel of Christ.* ⁸*But even if we or an angel from heaven should preach a gospel other than the one we preached to you, let him be eternally condemned!* ⁹*As we have already said, so now I say again: If anybody is preaching to you a gospel other than what you accepted, let him be eternally condemned!*

¹⁰*Am I now trying to win the approval of men, or of God? Or am I trying to please men? If I were still trying to please men, I would not be a servant of Christ.*

Group Questions

Every group meeting has three goals: **(1) To Begin** (15 Minutes) to break the ice; **(2) Read Scripture and Discuss** (30 Minutes); and **(3) To Close and Pray** (15–30 Minutes). Try to keep on schedule. The most important time is the prayer time.

TO BEGIN / 15 Minutes (Choose 1 or 2)

❑ In high school, how loyal were (are) your friends to you? How loyal were (are) you to them?
❑ In major purchases (like vehicles), do you typically switch manufacturers or stay with the same one?
❑ When you're upset with someone, do you usually give them a long lecture, a "piece of your mind," or the "silent treatment"?

READ SCRIPTURE AND DISCUSS / 30 Minutes

❑ How would you feel if a preacher began a sermon the way Paul begins the heart of this letter?
❑ How would the leaders of your church feel?
❑ What kind of "gospel" was being preached by those who Paul contends had led the Galatians astray? (Read the first two paragraphs of "The Issue" on the bottom of page 34.)
❑ How does Paul feel about the Judaizers' message that God still requires Christians to keep the Old Testament Law, such as circumcision (see vv. 6–7)?
❑ What does Paul say will happen to anyone who promotes a "gospel" other than that which Paul preached—the good news of grace (vv. 8–9)?
❑ How concerned is Paul about the effect of his strong words on these churches in Galatia, which he had previously founded (v. 10)?
❑ Who has been an "apostle Paul" in your life— someone who has made a significant contribution to your spiritual beginning or growth?
❑ Did your "apostle" ever need to straighten you out? What were the circumstances? How did you respond?
❑ Have you ever "deserted" God—"the one who called you by the grace of Christ"? What happened?
❑ How faithful to Christ and his Gospel are you now?

TO CLOSE AND PRAY / 15–30 Minutes

❑ If you were to describe the past week with a number between 1 and 10—1 being TERRIBLE and 10 being GREAT—what number would you choose? Why?
❑ How comfortable are you sharing your spiritual life and struggles with this group?
❑ Did you invite anyone to join the group this week?
❑ How can this group pray for you this week?

Notes

1:6–10 Paul points out that there is only one version of the Gospel and he is astounded that the Galatians should depart from it, regardless of who the proclaimer might be. Such distorters are worthy of condemnation. For his part, he refuses to tailor his message to the whims of the audience.

1:6 *astonished.* Typically at this place in a letter, Paul would commend the church (e.g., Rom. 1:8; Phil. 1:3). But here he skips the praise altogether and launches straight into his remonstration, expressing indignation at the news that they have been persuaded by the teaching of the Judaizers. *so quickly.* Paul has scarcely returned from his first missionary journey and already the Galatians are turning away from the truth. *deserting.* The word means, literally, a removal from one place to another, as for example the bones of Abraham from Egypt to Sechem (Acts 7:16). The word can also be used for those who "change sides"—for example, army deserters. *called.* It was God who beckoned them to salvation and from whom they are now defecting (though Paul's opponents would not have seen it that way, preferring to think that they were calling people to the true way). *grace.* This pinpoints the nature of their *turning*—from a gospel of unmerited favor to a gospel of works. *gospel.* The proclamation of the good news that in the life, death, and resurrection of Jesus, the kingdom of God has been made manifest and is open to all who by faith trust in his atoning work on the cross.

1:7 *no gospel.* A different gospel is really no gospel at all. It does not merit description as "good news." To be thrown back into bondage to the Law is, indeed, "bad news." *throwing you into confusion.* Some people are "troubling" the Galatians, "disturbing the peace" that ought to be found in the Gospel. The root word probably means seditious activity that would lead to desertion. *pervert.* The nature of the perversion will be made clear in chapter 5: male Gentile converts are being urged to be circumcised as a precondition for acceptance by God. "This word means to transfer to a different opinion, hence to change the essential character of a thing. ... The idea is not merely a twisting of the Gospel, but of giving it an emphasis which is virtually transformed into something else" (Guthrie).

1:8 What is crucial is the message, not the messenger. No matter who the messenger may be, that person and that message is to be rejected if it is different from that which brought salvation to the Galatians. It

is the *Gospel of Christ,* not the Gospel of Paul or anyone else. *eternally condemned.* The Greek word is *anathema* and is related to the Hebrew idea of the "ban," i.e., that which is set apart to God, usually for destruction. It stands as the direct opposite to God's grace, and is used by Paul as a solemn calling down of judgment on these Judaizers.

1:10 *now ... still.* There is an implied criticism of Paul here. Apparently he was being charged with vacillation—saying one thing here, another there; acting this way now, but in a different fashion elsewhere. "Who can trust that sort of person?" the Judaizers would have been saying. But as Paul points out, his anathema in verse 9 is certainly not the language of a man-pleaser! *win the approval.* Literally, "persuade." In fact, Paul understood his mission to be one of persuasion (see 2 Cor. 5:11), i.e., to urge man and woman to be reconciled to God (2 Cor. 5:20). But while it was his role to persuade human beings, it was not his job to persuade God. In fact, the very thought was abhorrent. God was God and his will reigned. Only religious charlatans claimed to a superstitious audience that they could change God's mind. *please men.* Men-pleasing (i.e., shifting his message and methods to gain their approval) was abhorrent to Paul (1 Thess. 2:4–6). So what Paul is saying is "that he persuades men, not God, and pleases God, not men; indeed, he pleases God by persuading men" (Bruce).

UNIT 3—Paul Called by God / Galatians 1:11–24

Scripture

Paul Called by God

¹¹I want you to know, brothers, that the gospel I preached is not something that man made up. ¹²I did not receive it from any man, nor was I taught it; rather, I received it by revelation from Jesus Christ.

¹³For you have heard of my previous way of life in Judaism, how intensely I persecuted the church of God and tried to destroy it. ¹⁴I was advancing in Judaism beyond many Jews of my own age and was extremely zealous for the traditions of my fathers. ¹⁵But when God, who set me apart from birth^a and called me by his grace, was pleased ¹⁶to reveal his Son in me so that I might preach him among the Gentiles, I did not consult any man, ¹⁷nor did I go up to Jerusalem to see those who were apostles before I was, but I went immediately into Arabia and later returned to Damascus.

¹⁸Then after three years, I went up to Jerusalem to get acquainted with Peter^b and stayed with him fifteen days. ¹⁹I saw none of the other apostles—only James, the Lord's brother. ²⁰I assure you before God that what I am writing you is no lie. ²¹Later I went to Syria and Cilicia. ²²I was personally unknown to the churches of Judea that are in Christ. ²³They only heard the report: "The man who formerly persecuted us is now preaching the faith he once tried to destroy." ²⁴And they praised God because of me.

Group Questions

Every group meeting has three goals: **(1) To Begin** (15 Minutes) to break the ice; **(2) Read Scripture and Discuss** (30 Minutes); and **(3) To Close and Pray** (15–30 Minutes). Try to keep on schedule. The most important time is the prayer time.

TO BEGIN / 15 Minutes (Choose 1 or 2)

❑ What "make believe" games did you play as a child?
❑ When you were in grade school, what did you want to be when you grew up?
❑ How important is it to you to consult others on major decisions you make?

READ SCRIPTURE AND DISCUSS / 30 Minutes

❑ How do you think the Galatians felt as they heard these words? (Remember, they didn't realize Paul was writing Scripture.) Would they have felt Paul was bordering on arrogance? Why or why not?
❑ In a letter of correction like this, how significant is it that Paul still refers to the Galatians as "brothers" (see Note on v. 11)?
❑ How was Paul's life changed?
❑ By whom (and what) was Paul called (v. 15)? What was he specifically called to do (v. 16)?
❑ Why did Paul stress the fact that he functioned independently from others: He was a "lone ranger" personality type? He didn't want the Judaizers to be able to say he had strayed from "apostolic" teaching about keeping the Law? He wanted the Galatians to understand he wasn't just passing on second-hand information, but had a real encounter with Christ on the Damascus road?
❑ If you had to argue for the reality of the Gospel by giving one example of how you have changed as a result of your faith, what would you share?
❑ How do you include your personal experience of Christ changing your life in your witness to others?

TO CLOSE AND PRAY / 15–30 Minutes

❑ How do you feel about your spiritual life in general, and your unique calling to serve God and others in particular?
❑ Is this group living up to your expectations? How could you improve it?
❑ How can your "brothers and sisters" lift you up in prayer this week?

---

^a15 Or *from my mother's womb*   ^b18 Greek *Cephas*

Notes

1:11–2:21 Paul recounts how he came to be an apostle, as he seeks to defend himself against the charge that he was not really an apostle and therefore unqualified to teach the true Gospel. His point is that his commission came directly from God (1:11–17), though later it was recognized by the leaders of the Jerusalem church (1:11–2:10). Furthermore, when at one point Peter seemed to capitulate to the vision of the Judaizers, Paul confronted him with his inconsistency (2:11–21).

1:11 Paul first states what the Gospel is not. It is not a product of intellectual musings, nor the conclusion of a philosophical system, nor even the logical outcome of centuries of Jewish thought. *brothers.* Paul's word for fellow Christians. Even though he has harsh words for the Galatians, they are still part of the family of faith. His words come with the awareness of this relationship, and are laced with love for them.

1:12 *revelation.* Lit.,"an opening up of what was previously hidden." Paul had certainly heard the "facts" of the Gospel prior to his conversion, but he had violently rejected them as blasphemous. It was only after Jesus Christ revealed the truth and meaning of these facts to him on the Damascus road that he accepted the Gospel.

1:13–17 Because he had been so zealous for Judaism, there was no one less likely than Paul to abandon the way of the Law. This could only have come about as the result of a direct revelation.

1:14 *traditions of my fathers.* In particular, the oral law developed over the years to explain and apply the OT, taught to Paul in the school of Gamaliel (Acts 22:3).

1:16 *among the Gentiles.* With Paul's conversion came also his commission to preach to the Gentiles (Acts 9:15). In encountering Christ, he came to the realization that the Law was bankrupt (insofar as its ability to save anyone). Thus there was no barrier preventing Gentiles from coming to the all-sufficient Christ.

1:17 Apparently the Judaizers had been saying that after his conversion Paul had gone to Jerusalem and there received instructions about the Gospel (including the requirement to be circumcised), but then later Paul went his own way and started teaching a law-free Gospel. *apostles before I was.* The only distinc-

tion Paul admits between his apostleship and that of the leaders in Jerusalem is that of time. They were commissioned by Jesus earlier than he was. *Arabia.* The desert-like region to the east of Damascus was part of Arabia. In the tradition of OT prophets (and of Jesus after his baptism), Paul retreats into the desert for solitude and reflection. He probably also preached to the Gentiles there, both in the cities and to the wandering Bedouins. That he was actively at work in Arabia can be inferred from 2 Corinthians 11:32–33 (where it appears that he had somehow offended King Aretas, the ruler of Arabia, who sent representatives into Damascus to arrest him).

1:18–19 "Paul's first visit to Jerusalem was only after three years, it lasted only two weeks, and he saw only two apostles. It was, therefore, ludicrous to suggest that he obtained his gospel from the Jerusalem apostles" (Stott).

1:18 *Jerusalem.* It was a courageous act by Paul to return here—to his former friends who might well try to harm him (because of his conversion to Christianity), and to new friends who might not even receive him (because of their suspicions about him). *to get acquainted.* It was important that Paul come to know the leaders of the church, in particular Peter (who was its undisputed head). They, in turn, needed to hear a first-hand account of his conversion.

1:19 *James.* See Mark 6:3; Acts 1:14. James eventually became the leader of the Jerusalem church. He was a strict and orthodox Jew.

1:20 *I assure you.* The taking of oaths was discouraged unless absolutely necessary (which Paul considers this to be, as he defends the independence of this Gospel and the validity of his apostleship).

1:24 Even though the Judaizers in Galatia might be critical of Paul, the Christians in Judea praised God because of him.

UNIT 4—Paul Accepted by the Apostles / Galatians 2:1–10

Scripture

Paul Accepted by the Apostles

2 *Fourteen years later I went up again to Jerusalem, this time with Barnabas. I took Titus along also. ²I went in response to a revelation and set before them the gospel that I preach among the Gentiles. But I did this privately to those who seemed to be leaders, for fear that I was running or had run my race in vain. ³Yet not even Titus, who was with me, was compelled to be circumcised, even though he was a Greek. ⁴This matter arose because some false brothers had infiltrated our ranks to spy on the freedom we have in Christ Jesus and to make us slaves. ⁵We did not give in to them for a moment, so that the truth of the gospel might remain with you.*

⁶As for those who seemed to be important—whatever they were makes no difference to me; God does not judge by external appearance—those men added nothing to my message. ⁷On the contrary, they saw that I had been entrusted with the task of preaching the gospel to the Gentiles,ᵃ just as Peter had been to the Jews.ᵇ ⁸For God, who was at work in the ministry of Peter as an apostle to the Jews, was also at work in my ministry as an apostle to the Gentiles. ⁹James, Peterᶜ and John, those reputed to be pillars, gave me and Barnabas the right hand of fellowship when they recognized the grace given to me. They agreed that we should go to the Gentiles, and they to the Jews. ¹⁰All they asked was that we should continue to remember the poor, the very thing I was eager to do.

Group Questions

TO BEGIN / 15 Minutes (Choose 1 or 2)

❏ Who did you spy on when you were a kid?
❏ As you were growing up, what were your family's attitudes toward poor people?
❏ Are you the type of person who usually "goes with the crowd" or "does your own thing"?

READ SCRIPTURE AND DISCUSS / 30 Minutes

❏ As Paul goes before the leaders of the church in Jerusalem, what was his concern (see Note on v. 2)?
❏ The "false brothers" had caused some believers to become "slaves" (v. 4). To what?
❏ What was the outcome of this meeting? What did the Jerusalem leaders add to Paul's message (v. 6)?
❏ If Paul's converts had to become Jews to be Christians, what would that have done to Paul's ministry to the Gentiles (v. 2)? What would be different about the church today?
❏ What did the spiritual "pillars" of the Jerusalem church recognize about Paul (v. 9)?
❏ How is *grace* the key to the critical issue of Galatians in general, and this passage in particular?
❏ How does caring for the poor (v. 10) relate to proclaiming the Gospel of grace?
❏ Is the Gospel really a "free lunch"? What "good" is tempting for you to add to the Good News as a requirement for inclusion in the church?

TO CLOSE AND PRAY / 15–30 Minutes

❏ What was your spiritual life like this past week? Can you describe the week in a weather report, such as sunny and warm? Cold and foggy? Several straight days of rain? Other?
❏ How can the group support your spiritual life?
❏ What can you and your group do to "remember the poor"?
❏ How about a prayer request for you this week?

ᵃ7 Greek *uncircumcised*   ᵇ7 Greek *circumcised*, also in verses 8 and 9
ᶜ9 Greek *Cephas*, also in verses 11 and 14

Notes

2:1 *fourteen years later.* It is not clear whether Paul means 14 years after his conversion or after his first visit to Jerusalem. In any case, the significant factor is that Paul had little contact with the leaders in Jerusalem. He was not their missionary. He did not take orders from them. *I went up again.* In 14 years Paul made only two fleeting visits to Jerusalem. The first was for the purpose of meeting Peter. The second was necessary in order to deliver to the mother church a famine collection donated by Christians at Antioch. *Barnabas.* A Levite from Cyprus, whose name was actually Joseph but who had been nick-named Barnabas (Son of Encouragement) by the apostles, presumably because he was that sort of person (Acts 4:36). When the church in Jerusalem heard that a great number of people in Antioch had turned to Jesus, they sent Barnabas to verify what was happening. Barnabas in turn, having seen this to be an authentic work of God, sought out Paul in Tarsus and brought him back to Antioch, where the two of them labored together to establish the church (Acts 11:19–30). *Titus.* A Gentile Christian from Antioch. Titus became an important coworker with Paul (2 Cor. 2:12–13; 7:15–16; 8:6–24; 9:3–5; 12:18) and later was the recipient of a Pastoral Letter.

2:2 *in response to a revelation.* Paul makes it quite clear that it was God who told him to visit Jerusalem. It was not a matter of the leaders there calling him to account for his actions. *in vain.* Paul preached that Gentiles could become Christians without first becoming Jews, i.e., that there was one church made up of both Jews and Gentiles. If the leaders in Jerusalem disputed this, his 14 years of work would have been in vain.

2:3 This did not happen. Even Titus (an uncircumcised Gentile Christian) was accepted—fully—right in the heart of Jewish Christianity.

2:4 *freedom.* Jew and Gentile Christians freely mixed, eating together and having fellowship. This stood in stark contrast to the way Jews and Gentiles normally related.

2:5 *did not give in.* On another occasion, Paul did have Timothy circumcised "because of the Jews who lived in that area" (Acts 16:5), but Timothy's mother was Jewish and Paul never suggested that Jews not be circumcised.

2:6 *As for those.* Paul resumes the main thread of his argument (vv. 3–5 having been a parenthesis). *who seemed to be important.* This phrase (as well as those in v. 2—"seemed to be leaders," and v. 9—"reputed to be pillars") might be construed to imply disrespect on Paul's part. In fact, Paul intended nothing of the sort. These men were authentic leaders and well-respected. What might have concerned Paul is that some of the Judaizers were exalting the role and position of these men (while they downplayed his own). *makes no difference to me.* The difference between these men and Paul is that they were founding members of the church and he was a latecomer. Still, each of them received his commission directly from the Lord. *God does not judge by external appearances.* "God does not favor companions or relatives of the historical Jesus over someone, like Paul, who received his apostolic commission later" (Bruce). *added nothing.* "No question was raised, apparently, about the comparative contents of Paul's gospel and theirs, any more than the question was raised about Paul's authority to preach his gospel. His gospel was unexceptionable; his commission was undisputed: the agenda, we gather, concentrated on the demarcation of the respective spheres of service of the parties to the discussion" (Bruce).

2:7 *On the contrary.* In fact, they acknowledged his sphere of authority. *to the Gentiles.* Though Paul did on occasions evangelize Jews (Acts 9:15; 26:20) his major mission was to the Gentiles (Acts 22:21). *to the Jews.* Though on one occasion Peter evangelized Gentiles such as in the home of Cornelius (Acts 10:1–11:18; 15:7–9), this was the exception, not the rule. God used that particular occasion to teach Peter (and through him, the Church at Jerusalem) that he was doing a new and unexpected thing: God was calling Gentiles to be his people. Peter's mission—which he carried out with great effectiveness—was to reach his own people in Jerusalem and Judea (Acts 2:14–41; 3:12–26; 9:32).

2:10 *remember the poor.* In fact, this is why Paul and Barnabas had come to Jerusalem—to deliver an offering given by the Christians at Antioch. In later years, Paul continued to raise funds for relief in Jerusalem (Rom. 15:25–28; 1 Cor. 16:1–4; 2 Cor. 8:1–9:15).

UNIT 5—Paul Opposes Peter / Galatians 2:11–21

Scripture

Paul Opposes Peter

[11]When Peter came to Antioch, I opposed him to his face, because he was clearly in the wrong. [12]Before certain men came from James, he used to eat with the Gentiles. But when they arrived, he began to draw back and separate himself from the Gentiles because he was afraid of those who belonged to the circumcision group. [13]The other Jews joined him in his hypocrisy, so that by their hypocrisy even Barnabas was led astray.

[14]When I saw that they were not acting in line with the truth of the gospel, I said to Peter in front of them all, "You are a Jew, yet you live like a Gentile and not like a Jew. How is it, then, that you force Gentiles to follow Jewish customs?

[15]"We who are Jews by birth and not 'Gentile sinners' [16]know that a man is not justified by observing the law, but by faith in Jesus Christ. So we, too, have put our faith in Christ Jesus that we may be justified by faith in Christ and not by observing the law, because by observing the law no one will be justified.

[17]"If, while we seek to be justified in Christ, it becomes evident that we ourselves are sinners, does that mean that Christ promotes sin? Absolutely not! [18]If I rebuild what I destroyed, I prove that I am a lawbreaker. [19]For through the law I died to the law so that I might live for God. [20]I have been crucified with Christ and I no longer live, but Christ lives in me. The life I live in the body, I live by faith in the Son of God, who loved me and gave himself for me. [21]I do not set aside the grace of God, for if righteousness could be gained through the law, Christ died for nothing!"[a]

Group Questions

TO BEGIN / 15 Minutes (Choose 1 or 2)

❏ As a child, how willing were you to try new foods? How about now?
❏ Have you ever "told off" your parents or boss? Why? What was the outcome?
❏ How much slower do you drive when you know a police or patrol vehicle is nearby?

READ SCRIPTURE AND DISCUSS / 30 Minutes

❏ In the past, God had dramatically led Peter to break Jewish custom by fellowshipping and eating with Gentiles (see Note on v. 12). What causes Peter to reverse course now?
❏ How do you think Paul felt when even Barnabas, his missionary partner, gave in to the Judaizers?
❏ What would it take for you to stand up at a dinner party and rebuke the recognized leader of the whole church (v. 14)?
❏ When are you guilty of double standards? For instance, how do you communicate—probably by example—"Do as I say, not as I do"?
❏ Verse 16 is the key verse in this letter (see Note on v. 16). How would you explain this verse to a non-Christian, particularly one with high moral standards?
❏ In the Christian life, what dies and what gets resurrected (vv. 19–20)? How is that made possible?
❏ Applying the spiritual concept of v. 20, who is "alive" in your life right now—"I," or "Christ in me"?
❏ According to verse 21, if you can be in right standing with God through your own efforts—for example, by being a "good person"—what did Christ die for?
❏ If you are a self-made person who likes to see everyone pay their own way, how does this Gospel of undeserved grace strike you?

TO CLOSE AND PRAY / 15–30 Minutes

❏ The lives and ministries of spiritual "giants" like Martin Luther were changed through these concepts. Are you likewise "justified" and living "by faith in the Son of God"?
❏ What will it take to get your spiritual life turned on?
❏ How can this group help you and pray for you?

---

[a]21 Some interpreters end the quotation after verse 14.

Notes

2:11–15 Paul concludes his autobiographical sketch by recounting an incident in which he had to rebuke Peter for his inconsistency. This showed beyond a shadow of a doubt that Paul was not under the jurisdiction of the Jerusalem leaders.

2:12 *from James.* Though he eventually sided with Paul and the others in agreeing that Gentiles need not be bound by Jewish customs (Acts 15), James is clearly quite conservative on this issue. ***he used to eat.*** Eating together was a sign of fellowship and indeed strong evidence that Christians—regardless of racial identity—had been made one family, having acknowledged one Lord and shared in one baptism and in one communion table (Eph. 2:11–3:13). Peter's action in eating with Gentiles is consistent with his behavior after his vision at Joppa (Acts 10)—he was quite willing to visit Cornelius and eat with his family (Acts 10:28; 11:3). ***with Gentiles.*** Though not strictly forbidden by the Law of Moses, at this point in history Jews simply did not eat with Gentiles.

2:13 *even Barnabas.* This must have been the hardest blow of all for Paul—to see his close associate in the Gentile mission capitulate to the circumcision party.

2:14 *live like a Gentile.* By disregarding Jewish prohibitions. ***force Gentiles.*** The logic is impeccable. By what reasoning could a Jew (who felt free to disregard the rules and regulations himself) demand that a Gentile be bound by what he, the Jew, had forsaken?!

2:15–21 Paul now leaves his own story and moves into the core of his theological case. Here he states the crux of his argument. In chapters 3–4 he will expound, extend and explain the universal principle set down here.

2:16 The key verse in Galatians in which the two options are clearly delineated by Paul whereby people might think to obtain right standing before God: by their own activity in law-keeping, or by simple trust in Jesus. In fact, there is only one path to right standing, namely, faith in Christ. ***justified.*** Behind this word stands the image of Judgment Day. The Jew was preoccupied with how one obtained a positive verdict (justification) from God the Judge, with how one gained "right standing" before God. ***observing the law.*** The Law is the sum of God's commandments. The Jews supposed that by keeping the Law, they could obtain right standing (justification) before God.

by faith. Right standing before God is made possible because of the death of Christ (not the *work* of any individual person), and the benefits of his death are appropriated simply by faith. ***in Jesus Christ.*** It is not *faith* in general that saves, but *faith in* a particular person. The person who has faith in *Jesus Christ* is the person who accepts that in the life, death, and resurrection of Jesus Christ one sees the power of God at work.

2:17 Verses 17–18 are difficult to understand. Paul may mean that when law-abiding Jews like he and Peter turn to Christ for justification, they de facto become like the *Gentile sinners* (v. 15). ***Christ promotes sin.*** In the sense that now all those law-abiding Jews are shown, in fact, to be *sinners,* and so the sheer number of sinners increases.

2:19 Paul seems to be saying that he cannot be a lawbreaker because he has died in relationship to the Law. He no longer lives in the sphere where the Law is operative (i.e., Judaism).

2:20 *I have been crucified with Christ.* On the Damascus road when Christ met him, "the old Paul died—not only the cruel little persecutor of the Christians, hating himself for it as we may surmise, but also the virtuous Pharisee who knew that his virtue was a hollow pretense, the godly rabbi who knew that his inner life was a travesty of what he professed in public" (Neil). ***I no longer live.*** Paul died in relationship to the Law. ***Christ lives in me.*** That which now activates the believer is the resurrection life and power of Jesus. ***I live by faith.*** Faith is that which bonds together the believer and the risen Christ. Paul will also refer to this as *living by the Spirit* (5:25).

2:21 *set aside the grace of God.* This was the error of the Judaizers. ***righteousness.*** In Hebrew thought, righteousness is not so much a moral quality as it is a legal judgment. A person is *counted* or *reckoned* as righteous (even though they are really guilty). They are *pardoned.* They are given right standing before God, by *grace* operating through the death of Christ. ***Christ died for nothing.*** This is the conclusion of his argument against the Judaizers. If they were right, Christ died for nothing.

UNIT 6—Faith or Observance of the Law / Galatians 3:1–14

Scripture

Faith or Observance of the Law

3 *You foolish Galatians! Who has bewitched you? Before your very eyes Jesus Christ was clearly portrayed as crucified. ²I would like to learn just one thing from you: Did you receive the Spirit by observing the law, or by believing what you heard? ³Are you so foolish? After beginning with the Spirit, are you now trying to attain your goal by human effort? ⁴Have you suffered so much for nothing—if it really was for nothing? ⁵Does God give you his Spirit and work miracles among you because you observe the law, or because you believe what you heard?*

⁶Consider Abraham: "He believed God, and it was credited to him as righteousness."ᵃ ⁷Understand, then, that those who believe are children of Abraham. ⁸The Scripture foresaw that God would justify the Gentiles by faith, and announced the gospel in advance to Abraham: "All nations will be blessed through you."ᵇ ⁹So those who have faith are blessed along with Abraham, the man of faith.

¹⁰All who rely on observing the law are under a curse, for it is written: "Cursed is everyone who does not continue to do everything written in the Book of the Law."ᶜ ¹¹Clearly no one is justified before God by the law, because, "The righteous will live by faith."ᵈ ¹²The law is not based on faith; on the contrary, "The man who does these things will live by them."ᵉ ¹³Christ redeemed us from the curse of the law by becoming a curse for us, for it is written: "Cursed is everyone who is hung on a tree."ᶠ ¹⁴He redeemed us in order that the blessing given to Abraham might come to the Gentiles through Christ Jesus, so that by faith we might receive the promise of the Spirit.

Group Questions

TO BEGIN / 15 Minutes (Choose 1 or 2)

- ❑ Have you ever been "dropped" by someone you were dating? What did that do to your emotions?
- ❑ What physical or personality traits have been passed on to you from your family?
- ❑ How do you feel when someone you love does something foolish? What do you typically do?

READ SCRIPTURE AND DISCUSS / 30 Minutes

- ❑ To what extent was the Galatians' conversion experience related to observing the Law?
- ❑ Why would anyone revert from a liberating spiritual life of faith to a legalistic spiritual life of works and "performance"?
- ❑ When have you gone in that direction? What caused it to happen?
- ❑ Was Abraham considered righteous by God through his faith or through his works (vv. 6–9)?
- ❑ Who are the true children of Abraham? Who is eligible to be one?
- ❑ What "additions" to faith might outsiders sense in your Christian circles regarding what they should do to be approved? How can you help break down these barriers?
- ❑ How do the principles and quotations from the Old Testament (vv. 10–12) highlight the problem that no one can earn their right standing with God?
- ❑ How does Jesus solve this problem for us (vv. 13–14)?
- ❑ Are you walking in the blessings of the Spirit available to the children of Abraham? Why or why not?

TO CLOSE AND PRAY / 15–30 Minutes

- ❑ What kind of TV show has your life been like this week? A soap opera? A comedy? A heavy drama?
- ❑ What do you need this week to help you switch to a better channel?
- ❑ How could this group help you in prayer to do so?

ᵃ6 Gen. 15:6   ᵇ8 Gen. 12:3; 18:18; 22:18   ᶜ10 Deut. 27:26   ᵈ11 Hab. 2:4   ᵉ12 Lev. 18:5   ᶠ13 Deut. 21:23

Notes

3:1 foolish. Paul's feelings of exasperation and indignation flare up. How could they have been so *stupid* (as the NEB translates the word)? It is not that they were unable to understand what was happening. They simply failed to use their minds.

3:2 Paul asks them to recall that their conversion experience had nothing to do with observing the Law. The gift of the Spirit—assumed to be the most significant experience a person can have—came by faith. Once this is noted, nothing further need be said about the inadequacy of law-keeping. *I would like to learn just one thing.* If they concede this, Paul's whole argument must be accepted. *receive the Spirit.* Faith in Christ brings both justification (2:16) and the gift of the Spirit.

3:3 Could they actually believe that *spiritual life* had anything to do with the observance of *human* customs and laws? *foolish.* Their immature return to legalistic obedience to the Law (when they know by what means they received the Spirit) justifies Paul's use of this strong adjective.

3:4 suffered. We are never told about the nature of their persecution, but the implication here is that they had suffered for their faith (all of which would have been pointless if they could have received salvation simply by circumcision and law-keeping). Why then suffer as a result of following the crucified Christ?

3:5 miracles. Extraordinary things happened in the early Christian church: lives were changed, people were healed (Acts 14:8–10), demons were cast out, some (like Dorcas) were even restored to life (Acts 9:32–43). The Galatians actually experienced the power of the Holy Spirit. All this stood in sharp contrast to their experiences as pagan idol-worshipers.

3:6-9 Paul turns from his argument based on their experience to an argument based on OT Scripture. Here he shows that it has always been by faith that men and women became God's children.

3:6 he believed God. God promised Abraham descendants as numerous as the stars, even though his wife Sarah was barren! Despite the improbability of this ever happening, Abraham still trusted God that it would be so. *credited ... as righteousness.* For Abraham, right standing before God came by faith, not by law-keeping in general (or circumcision in particular).

3:7–9 children of Abraham. The real sons and daughters of Abraham are not those who are his racial descendants, but those who believe—be they Jew or Gentile.

3:8 announced the gospel in advance. The promise to Abraham foreshadowed the Gospel and is only fulfilled in the Gospel. This is how Paul can use passages from Genesis to prove his point: there is continuity between Abraham's faith and the faith of Christians (John 8:56).

3:9 blessed. Not only are people of faith sons and daughters of Abraham, but they also share in the blessings which were promised to Abraham.

3:10–14 Paul's next point (which he makes via a string of OT quotes) is that law-keeping is ultimately futile, because no one is able to fulfill the *whole* Law—therefore no one is justified by the Law. Rather a curse hangs heavy upon them. Blessing comes by faith.

3:10 According to Deuteronomy 27:26, anyone not keeping the *whole* Law is accursed. *under a curse.* That is, separated from God. This curse is the opposite of the blessing promised in verse 9. *it is written.* Paul continues to evoke the authority of Scripture.

3:11 In verse 6 Paul argued that Abraham was justified by faith. "But was he not a special case?" it might be asked. Here Paul cites the same principle, given as a universal truth: right standing before God comes by faith.

3:12 There is no connection between Law and faith. Law requires obedience, not belief.

3:13 The only way to escape the curse laid upon a person by dint of personal (and inevitable) failure to keep the whole Law is by having another bear that curse for you. Since Christ had kept the whole Law (he was without sin), he had no curse on himself and so could bear the curse of others. He was "made sin for us" (as Paul says in 2 Cor. 5:21).

UNIT 7—The Law and the Promise / Galatians 3:15–25

Scripture

The Law and the Promise

¹⁵Brothers, let me take an example from everyday life. Just as no one can set aside or add to a human covenant that has been duly established, so it is in this case. ¹⁶The promises were spoken to Abraham and to his seed. The Scripture does not say "and to seeds," meaning many people, but "and to your seed,"^a meaning one person, who is Christ. ¹⁷What I mean is this: The law, introduced 430 years later, does not set aside the covenant previously established by God and thus do away with the promise. ¹⁸For if the inheritance depends on the law, then it no longer depends on a promise; but God in his grace gave it to Abraham through a promise.

¹⁹What, then, was the purpose of the law? It was added because of transgressions until the Seed to whom the promise referred had come. The law was put into effect through angels by a mediator. ²⁰A mediator, however, does not represent just one party; but God is one.

²¹Is the law, therefore, opposed to the promises of God? Absolutely not! For if a law had been given that could impart life, then righteousness would certainly have come by the law. ²²But the Scripture declares that the whole world is a prisoner of sin, so that what was promised, being given through faith in Jesus Christ, might be given to those who believe.

²³Before this faith came, we were held prisoners by the law, locked up until faith should be revealed. ²⁴So the law was put in charge to lead us to Christ^b that we might be justified by faith. ²⁵Now that faith has come, we are no longer under the supervision of the law.

Group Questions

TO BEGIN / 15 Minutes (Choose 1 or 2)

❑ When you think of babysitters you had when you were growing up, who comes to mind? How did you feel about that person?
❑ In your family, how far back can you trace your spiritual roots?
❑ How important do you think it is for people to have a will?

READ SCRIPTURE AND DISCUSS / 30 Minutes

❑ In what way is the human covenant of a will like God's covenant-promise with Abraham and his seed (v. 15)?
❑ Who is *the* Seed through whom the promise to Abraham will be fulfilled (see Note on v. 16)?
❑ Since the Law was not to take the place of the promise, what was its purpose? Did God intend for the Law to be temporary or permanent (see Note on v. 19)?
❑ Can the Old Testament Law give "life" (v. 21)? Who can? How (v. 22)?
❑ How is attempting to be right with God through keeping the Law like being in prison (v. 23)? Like having a babysitter (see Note on vv. 24–25)?
❑ How would you share this passage with someone who thinks keeping the Ten Commandments or Golden Rule is enough to be right with God? Or to someone who was brought up believing that keeping rules wins approval?
❑ How has, and is, your faith liberating you from this spiritual bondage?
❑ Have you grown out of your need for rules to be your "babysitter"?

TO CLOSE AND PRAY / 15–30 Minutes

❑ What motivates your spiritual life? If there were no eternal rewards to be gained, would it still be worth it?
❑ If you had to miss the next session of this study, what would you miss the most about this group?
❑ What is keeping your group from doubling?
❑ How can the group hold you up in prayer this week?

^a*16* Gen. 12:7; 13:15; 24:7   ^b*24* Or *charge until Christ came*

Notes

3:15–18 Having argued from experience and from Scripture for the primacy of faith, Paul now argues the same point from human reason. He asks the Galatians to think about how wills are made. His point is that once established, no one can alter a will. Likewise, the covenant given by God to Abraham cannot be altered. So the Law which was given to Moses several centuries later has no impact on this covenant-promise. The promised blessings came to Abraham's true children, not because they earned them via law-keeping (there is no legal right here), but because they came by grace without conditions.

3:15 *an example.* In his appeal to reason, Paul points to judicial practices by way of analogy. A will cannot be annulled by law. *no one can set aside.* "When a deed of settlement is properly signed, sealed, and delivered and the property legally conveyed, not even the original owner can revoke or alter its terms" (Bruce). *or add to.* Under Roman law a "testator could add a codicil at any time that he chose, but after his death (or before it, for that matter) nobody else might do so" (Bruce). *covenant.* Akin to a last will and testament in which one's descendants are promised certain things. In this case the blessings promised to the children of Abraham are, according to Paul, justification by faith and the gift of the Spirit (vv. 10–14).

3:16 A point of grammar introduces a key distinction. God's promises to Abraham were not for *all* his many descendants, but more specifically, for his one crucial descendant: the Messiah. The blessings are then channeled outward to all who believe—Jew or Gentile—through Jesus the Messiah.

3:17 The prior covenant is unaffected by the later Law. *430 years later.* The Law was given much later, during the time of Moses.

3:18 *inheritance.* Promises made to a person's descendants. *grace.* God's promises to Abraham had nothing to do with law or obligations. It was pure gift without conditions.

3:19 *the law?* If the promises came by faith, what about the Law? What purpose did it have? This is a burning question to the Judaizers (for whom the Law was their whole life), because they felt that it reflected perfectly God's will. *it was added ... until.* Paul answers that the Law was *temporary*. Its purpose was to make people aware of their sin, but when the Messiah came its function would cease. "That the pro-

mulgation of specific enactments creates a corresponding category of specific violations, with opportunity (and perhaps temptation) to commit these violations, is a fact of human experience. But Paul's statement goes beyond this: the *purpose* of the law was to increase the sum-total of transgression" (Bruce). *by a mediator.* On the basis of Deuteronomy 33:2, it was concluded that the Law was given to Moses at Mt. Sinai by the angels who accompanied God. Paul's point is that a word that came indirectly from God is of less significance than one that came directly, as did God's promises to Abraham.

3:21 The Law and the promises (Moses and Abraham) are *not* in opposition. But Paul knew as a former Pharisee that the Law could not and did not impart *life.* The promised life only came by faith. "Paul's method of reasoning appears to be as follows. Law is associated with curses, the very antithesis of life. Law, in fact, could only show that man did not qualify for life. It has no power to bring to life that which it had pronounced dead. That is because it is contrary to the nature of law to give life ... (Paul's) purpose is to show that the reasons for the superiority of promise over law is not due to any failure on the part of the latter to achieve what it was designed to do. It had brought no life because it had never been intended for that purpose" (Guthrie). *life.* Spiritual life flows out of right relationship to God and this does not come about as a result of observing the Law, no matter how true that law might be. If the Law could give life, Christ didn't need to die (2:21).

3:24–25 The Law cannot impart life, but it does reveal the bondage of people to sin and thus drives them to faith as their only hope. *put in charge.* The Law is now pictured as a tutor. The same word was used for household slaves whose responsibility it was to look after the young men in the family until they reached the age of accountability. Such "tutors" were more involved in discipline than education, however. The Law functioned in the same way. It "looked after us" until Christ came, whereupon its task was finished.

UNIT 8—Sons of God / Galatians 3:26–4:7

Scripture

Sons of God

26You are all sons of God through faith in Christ Jesus, 27for all of you who were baptized into Christ have clothed yourselves with Christ. 28There is neither Jew nor Greek, slave nor free, male nor female, for you are all one in Christ Jesus. 29If, you belong to Christ, then you are Abraham's seed, and heirs according to the promise.

4 *What I am saying is that as long as the heir is a child, he is no different from a slave, although he owns the whole estate. 2He is subject to guardians and trustees until the time set by his father. 3So also, when we were children, we were in slavery under the basic principles of the world. 4But when the time had fully come, God sent his Son, born of a woman, born under law, 5to redeem those under law, that we might receive the full rights of sons. 6Because you are sons, God sent the Spirit of his Son into our hearts, the Spirit who calls out, "Abba,ª Father." 7So you are no longer a slave, but a son; and since you are a son, God has made you also an heir.*

Group Questions

TO BEGIN / 15 Minutes (Choose 1 or 2)

❏ When you were born, were you early, late or "on time"?
❏ Are you usually early, late or on time in your arrivals now? What about to this Bible study?
❏ How affectionate was, or is, your relationship with your parents?

READ SCRIPTURE AND DISCUSS / 30 Minutes

❏ What does it take to become a child of God?
❏ What effect does being "in Christ" have on relationships among believers (v. 28)?
❏ How much have people and their attitudes *really* changed since the New Testament times (see Note on v. 28 regarding first-century social barriers)?
❏ What are some social and cultural barriers in our time? Should we expect to experience unity between Christians of these different groups today, or do we have to wait until we get to heaven?
❏ What can you do to increase the sense of oneness in Christ in your sphere of influence? In your church? In this group?
❏ How is being under the Law like being an heir who is still a minor (vv. 1–3)?
❏ How has God intervened to alter human history and adopt us as full heirs (vv. 4–5)? (See Note on v. 4 to help appreciate God's marvelous plan and timing.)
❏ What further benefit does God give to his children (v. 6)?
❏ Do you feel more like a "slave" or a "son"? Is your heart filled more with frustration or with the fellowship of God's Spirit?

TO CLOSE AND PRAY / 15–30 Minutes

❏ How affectionate is your relationship with God right now: Very close, like a child and his/her Daddy (or "Abba"—v. 6)? Sort of close, like a parent and grown child who just "keep in touch"? Strained, like a parent and child who have had a "falling out"?
❏ How warm is your heart toward others "in Christ Jesus"?
❏ How can this group pray for you in these or other areas?

ª6 Aramaic for *Father*

Notes

3:26 *sons of God.* With the advent of faith (v. 25) came a whole new possibility: to become a child of God in a real, immediate way. ***in Christ Jesus.*** A distinctive Pauline phrase by which he seeks to express the faith-union between Jesus and the believer. This includes but transcends mere affirmation on a cognitive level that Jesus is Lord of the Universe. There is also an inner, mystical experience both for individual believers and for the Christian community as a whole.

3:28 *Jew or Greek.* From the first-century Jewish perspective, the cleavage between Jew and Greek was of the deepest sort. Jewish contempt for non-Jews was immense. Gentiles, they said, had been created by God as fuel for the fires of hell. For that barrier to have fallen was simply incredible. ***slave or free.*** Although the some 60 million slaves virtually ran the Roman Empire, they were generally regarded as mere things, without rights, subject to any whim of their masters. This was another barrier broken down by Christ. ***male or female.*** A woman had few if any rights in either first-century Judaism or Graeco-Roman culture. She belonged to her husband and he could treat her as he chose, including divorcing her with ease. This barrier, too, Christ removed so that in the same way a Gentile or a slave could exercise leadership in the church, so too could women. ***one in Christ Jesus.*** In morning prayer, a Jewish man thanked God that he had not been made a Gentile, a slave, or a woman. (The idea was not to disparage such people, but to express gratitude to God that as a man, he was not disqualified as they were from certain religious privileges.) Paul reverses this prayer. The traditional distinctions are finished. In Christ all are one. This was a radical principle in his time (and ours) when deep division was rife. It serves as a universal statement of what is meant to be.

4:1–2 The child is heir to the whole estate but in fact he is no better off than a slave (because he is under the strict control of his guardian and has no access to the inheritance). ***guardians and trustees.*** In his will, a Roman father appointed a guardian who looked after the child until he came of age at 14. Then a curator looked after the child's affairs until age 25. ***until the time set.*** The father had some discretion as to when the child received the inheritance.

4:4 *when the time had fully come.* Finally the long history of God's revelation reaches a culminating point: Jesus is sent. In fact it was the perfect point in history for such an event. For the first time the whole world was at peace, united under one power—Rome. There was a common tongue—Greek; and a network of first-rate roads spanning the Empire so that the message could spread. There was also widespread anxiety and questing for truth—the temple cults and philosophical systems having shown themselves to be barren of meaning. Therefore the message would be heard eagerly. ***born of a woman.*** The God of the Universe, incredibly, sends his own divine, unique Son down through time and space into history as a human baby. The divine invades the natural. ***born under the law.*** Not only did the Son experience the humiliation of Incarnation (he was born), but also the frustration of bondage to the very Law from which he came to free humanity.

4:5 *to redeem those under the law.* His purpose was to release the prisoners, to free the slaves, to bear the curse of the Law himself. Jesus delivered people from the Law to son/daughtership. ***full rights of sons.*** Lit., adoption, a wide-spread practice in the Graeco-Roman world whereby a child became a member of a new family with equivalent rights to those born in the family.

4:6 *sent the Spirit.* To become a child of God means that a person receives the Spirit of God; to one's new, external status is added new, internal experience of God's love and power. ***Abba.*** The Aramaic word for father—literally, "Daddy." The adoptive children are not bound in a mere legal sense to this new Father; but a deep, affectionate relationship exists.

4:7 *slave/son.* The Christian is no longer enslaved by the powers (v. 3) but is freed to become a son or daughter of God. His/Her status changes from slave to child. ***heir.*** As a child of God, one is the inheritor of all his promised blessings.

UNIT 9—Paul's Concern for the Galatians / Galatians 4:8–20

Scripture

Paul's Concern for the Galatians

⁸*Formerly, when you did not know God, you were slaves to those who by nature are not gods. ⁹But now that you know God—or rather are known by God—how is it that you are turning back to those weak and miserable principles? Do you wish to be enslaved by them all over again? ¹⁰You are observing special days and months and seasons and years! ¹¹I fear for you, that somehow I have wasted my efforts on you.*

¹²*I plead with you, brothers, become like me, for I became like you. You have done me no wrong. ¹³As you know, it was because of an illness that I first preached the gospel to you. ¹⁴Even though my illness was a trial to you, you did not treat me with contempt or scorn. Instead, you welcomed me as if I were an angel of God, as if I were Christ Jesus himself. ¹⁵What has happened to all your joy? I can testify that, if you could have done so, you would have torn out your eyes and given them to me. ¹⁶Have I now become your enemy by telling you the truth?*

¹⁷*Those people are zealous to win you over, but for no good. What they want is to alienate you from us, so that you may be zealous for them. ¹⁸It is fine to be zealous, provided the purpose is good, and to be so always and not just when I am with you. ¹⁹My dear children, for whom I am again in the pains of childbirth until Christ is formed in you, ²⁰how I wish I could be with you now and change my tone, because I am perplexed about you!*

Group Questions

TO BEGIN / 15 Minutes (Choose 1 or 2)

❑ How much joy did you have in the beginning phase of your Christian life?
❑ What is one of your most compulsive habits? How are you trying to break it?
❑ How do you relate to someone close to you whom you're worried about? How does your tone of voice change when you talk to them?

READ SCRIPTURE AND DISCUSS / 30 Minutes

❑ Prior to their conversion, the Galatians worshiped pagan gods that were in reality not gods (v. 8). How are they now doing the same thing with Jewish observances (see Note on v. 10)?
❑ How does Paul express the following emotions as he writes these words: Personal frustration mixed with concern (v. 11)? Pleading (v. 12)? Nostalgia (vv. 13–15)? Self-pity (v. 16)? Jealousy (v. 17)? Compassion (v. 19)? Anxiety (v. 20)?
❑ Overall, was Paul more concerned for himself or the Galatians?
❑ How would you like for Paul to be your "apostle"?
❑ If the first time Paul felt the "pains of childbirth" (v. 19) was for the Galatians' deliverance from pagan sin, what do they need to be "delivered" from this time (see Note on v. 19)?
❑ How has your relationship with God changed from being one based on zealous love and trust to one based on "performance" and keeping the rules?
❑ Like the Galatians, have you slipped back into any bad habits or old ways, from which Christ once delivered you? Which ones? What can you do about it?

TO CLOSE AND PRAY / 15–30 Minutes

❑ In the words of Paul, "What has happened to all your joy" (v. 15)? On a scale of 1 (lowest) to 10 (highest), how much joy is in your life?
❑ What effort can your group make to help people in your neighborhood or community "know God" and be "known by God"?
❑ How can the group continue to pray for you?

Notes

4:8 you. Now Paul addresses specifically the Gentile Christians in Galatia. **are not gods.** In their pagan days they worshiped many entities (idols, animals, powers) that really were not gods.

4:9 are known. To know God is to be known by God—the relationship is reciprocal. By this phrase he also emphasizes that it was nothing the Gentiles did that brought about such a relationship. God took the initiative. **turning back.** Paul can't imagine how they can turn from the experience of the living God to the bondage of pretend gods. **weak and miserable.** Although these powers were once strong enough to enslave a person, now because of Christ's liberating work they are rendered impotent—unless people deliberately put themselves back under their control. **principles.** The Gentiles, too, were under bondage to principles. This term was used to refer to the four physical elements—earth, air, fire and water. Since in the Greek worldview all such forces were understood to be animate, these principles came to be regarded as personal beings—angelic and demonic powers that were thought to rule the universe and influence the fate of individuals. Much pagan religion sought to tame and control these powerful entities.

4:10 The Jews were rigorous in observing days (like the Sabbath), months (e.g., the "new moons" in Isa. 1:14 and the offerings in Num. 28:11-15), seasons (e.g., Passover), and years (e.g., the sabbatical year in Lev. 25). "Since all these observations depend on astronomical calculations, they sprung in the last resort from the same kind of superstition as heathenism" (Neil). To observe such a sacred calendar is to put oneself once more under the power of the forces that control the calendar. **observing.** Paul observed certain sacred events (1 Cor. 16:8; Acts 20:16). But it is one thing for a Jew to continue in his ethnic tradition in a non-binding way, and another for a group of Gentiles to adopt in a legalistic fashion the Jewish calendar.

4:12–20 Paul breaks off the flow of his argument and makes a personal appeal to the Galatians.

4:12 become like me. When Paul was among them he was not bound by Jewish customs and practices. They, too, must avoid the trap of legalism. **I became like you.** "I came to count myself as one of you," perhaps he is referring to his willingness to become all things to all people in order to win them (1 Cor. 9:19–23). Certainly he did not live in a rigid, law-oriented way but was free to mingle in Gentile society. **done me no wrong.** Paul harbors no resentment. What he has written is out of concern for their Christian faith.

4:14 illness. Some take this to be malaria, believing that Paul had contracted it in the lowlands around Pamphylia and then made his way into the highlands of Pisidion Antioch (in Galatia) in order to recover (Acts 13:13–14). Others have identified his illness as epilepsy; still others as ophthalmia (because in v. 15 the Galatians would have given their eyes to him). However, there is no way to be certain about his ailment. **a trial to you.** For some reason the illness had made Paul repulsive in appearance. **scorn.** Literally, "to spit out." **an angel.** Perhaps there is an allusion to the time when Paul and Barnabas went to Lystra and were mistaken for gods (Acts 14:11–13). In any case, the contrast is between the greeting given an angel or Christ Jesus and their present attitude toward Paul.

4:15 torn out your eyes. Probably just an expression of deep gratitude; i.e., at that time there was nothing the Galatians would not have done for Paul.

4:16 In contrast to their original affection they are now treating Paul as an enemy.

4:17 The Judaizers are out to win adherents, even though by so doing they lure the Galatians from the true Gospel.

4:19 Paul often refers to himself as the father of spiritual children (1 Cor. 4:15). Here he plays the part of a mother, and so expresses his deep love and concern. **My dear children.** Paul cannot mask his deep affection for them despite his deep distress over their actions. **again.** For the second time he must endure the pangs of childbirth—first when he sought to bring them out of paganism and into new birth in Christ, and now as he seeks to bring their faith out of legalism. **Christ is found in you.** The metaphor is mixed but the point is clear. Paul's desire is that they come to possess Christlike characters.

UNIT 10—Hagar and Sarah / Galatians 4:21–31

Scripture

Hagar and Sarah

²¹Tell me, you who want to be under the law, are you not aware of what the law says? ²²For it is written that Abraham had two sons, one by the slave woman and the other by the free woman. ²³His son by the slave woman was born in the ordinary way; but his son by the free woman was born as the result of a promise.

²⁴These things may be taken figuratively, for the women represent two covenants. One covenant is from Mount Sinai and bears children who are to be slaves: This is Hagar. ²⁵Now Hagar stands for Mount Sinai in Arabia and corresponds to the present city of Jerusalem, because she is in slavery with her children. ²⁶But the Jerusalem that is above is free, and she is our mother. ²⁷For it is written:

"Be glad, O barren woman,
who bears no children;
break forth and cry aloud,
you who have no labor pains;
because more are the children of the
desolate woman
*than of her who has a husband."*ᵃ

*²⁸Now you, brothers, like Isaac, are children of promise. ²⁹At that time the son born in the ordinary way persecuted the son born by the power of the Spirit. It is the same now. ³⁰But what does the Scripture say? "Get rid of the slave woman and her son, for the slave woman's son will never share in the inheritance with the free woman's son."*ᵇ *³¹Therefore, brothers, we are not children of the slave woman, but of the free woman.*

Group Questions

TO BEGIN / 15 Minutes (Choose 1 or 2)

❑ What story do (or did) your parents tell about your birth?
❑ In books, movies, plays, etc. do you prefer entertaining, easy to follow plots—or complicated plots that don't make sense until the last scene?
❑ How would you like to be married to two women, or be the wife of a man with two wives?

READ SCRIPTURE AND DISCUSS / 30 Minutes

❑ What do you remember about the story in Genesis of Hagar and Sarah and their sons—Ishmael and Isaac (see Note on v. 22)?
❑ What was extraordinary about Isaac's birth (see Note on v. 23)?
❑ Normally, the Jews would regard Sarah as their spiritual mother and Hagar as the mother of the Gentiles. But which woman, figuratively speaking, does Paul say represents the covenant of Law given to the Jews through Moses on Mt. Sinai (v. 24)?
❑ Why does Paul turn the tables on this story and indicate that the Jews are actually the ones in slavery with Hagar—their slave woman mother (v. 25)?
❑ What does verse 27 say figuratively about Sarah's children? How did the spiritual and numerical growth of the Gentiles fulfill this Scripture from Isaiah?
❑ How does verse 30 give a stern warning to the Judaizers?
❑ Are you living like a "child of the free woman"—liberated from the bondage of trying to win God's approval? How can you live out your "freedom" in Christ, and still please him with your sacrificial obedience?

TO CLOSE AND PRAY / 15–30 Minutes

❑ Which sign would be appropriate right now for your spiritual life: Under new management? Out to lunch? Remodeling—Pardon the mess?
❑ What do you appreciate most about this group?
❑ How would you like this group to support you in prayer this week?

ᵃ27 Isaiah 54:1 ᵇ30 Gen. 21:10

Notes

4:21–31 Paul returns to his doctrinal argument. He does so by picking up the idea of childbirth (v. 19) and developing a complex allegory based on the experience of Hagar and Sarah and their two sons, Ishmael and Isaac. His main thesis is that Judaism is based on the Law, while Christianity is based on the promises of God. The Law brings slavery, while the promises if desired [of God] bring freedom.

4:21 *are you not aware.* If they insist on being under the Law, Paul wants them to be quite clear about the implications of this. Abraham had two sons. One was under bondage while the other was free. Paul will urge them to be like the child of the free woman and not be bound to the slavery of the Law.

4:22 *it is written.* Paul will make his case from Old Testament Scriptures. ***two sons.*** Sarah had failed to produce a son for Abraham and so decided to do so by proxy through her Egyptian servant, Hagar. This was, apparently, a recognized custom (Gen. 30:3–13). Ishmael was born in due course to the great delight of Abraham (Gen. 16:1–16; 17:18). However, some years later, God promised to give Abraham a son by Sarah and, indeed, a year later Isaac was born. When this happened, Sarah demanded that Abraham cast out Hagar and Ishmael. He did this with great distress, only after God promised that Ishmael would become the father of a great nation (the Arab tribes). The Ishmaelites eventually came to represent (for the Jews) all Gentiles—i.e., those excluded from God's covenants.

4:23 *in the ordinary way.* There was nothing exceptional about this birth. ***as the result of a promise.*** On the other hand, Isaac's birth was quite extraordinary; not at all to be expected in the course of nature. Both Abraham and Sarah were well beyond the age of childbearing.

4:24. *figuratively.* Literally, "as an allegory." An incident from the Old Testament is interpreted to have spiritual significance for the present because God is understood to operate in similar ways throughout history. Thus his action in Old Testament times prefigures his action in New Testament times. ***two covenants.*** The contrast is between Hagar (who represents the covenant of Law which was given to Moses on Mt. Sinai) and Sarah (who represents the covenant of promise given to Abraham). In contrast to the way the Judaizers understood the stories, the Jews were seen

by Paul as descending from Hagar (since they were enslaved by the Law), while the Gentiles (and a minority of believing Jews) were understood to be Sarah's descendants (since they had been liberated from the Law by Christ and were therefore free). ***covenant.*** A solemn agreement between God and people, in which he promises to be their God and they promise to be his people. The new covenant came through Christ. The old covenant was based on Law; the new on promises. In the old covenant, a heavy responsibility was placed on people to obey ("thou shalt not"), while in the new covenant the responsibility is God's ("I will") (Stott).

4:25 *the present city of Jerusalem.* For Paul, this represents contemporary Judaism with all its legalism. ***in slavery.*** Just as Jerusalem was in slavery to Rome, the Jews were enslaved to the Law which had become an enormous burden (expressed in a multitude of regulations covering every conceivable situation). ***Mt. Sinai.*** The mountain in Arabia upon which Moses received the Law.

4:26 *Jerusalem that is above.* The heavenly city that was thought to provide the pattern for the actual city. The heavenly Jerusalem is the real thing, uncorrupted, perfect (see also Heb. 12:22; Rev. 3:12; 21:2,9–14). Here it stands for the Christian church.

4:27 Isaiah was celebrating the fact that though the children of Zion (Jerusalem) had been carried into captivity in Babylon, one day they would return and become more numerous than before. So, too, the Gentiles were spiritually barren but are now producing spiritual fruit.

4:29 In 1 Thessalonians 2:14–16, Paul mentions Jewish persecution of Christians.

4:30 When Sarah sees Ishmael playing with Isaac, she recalls her jealousy of Hagar and so tells Abraham to drive them from the camp. Paul's point is that "legal bondage and spiritual freedom cannot coexist" (Bruce). Paul is not considering the question of Sarah's jealousy or her unkindness.

UNIT 11—Freedom in Christ / Galatians 5:1–15

Scripture

Freedom in Christ

5 *It is for freedom that Christ has set us free. Stand firm, then, and do not let yourselves be burdened again by a yoke of slavery.*

²Mark my words! I, Paul, tell you that if you let yourselves be circumcised, Christ will be of no value to you at all. ³Again I declare to every man who lets himself be circumcised that he is obligated to obey the whole law. ⁴You who are trying to be justified by law have been alienated from Christ; you have fallen away from grace. ⁵But by faith we eagerly await through the Spirit the right-eousness for which we hope. ⁶For in Christ Jesus neither circumcision nor uncircumci-sion has any value. The only thing that counts is faith expressing itself through love.

⁷You were running a good race. Who cut in on you and kept you from obeying the truth? ⁸That kind of persuasion does not come from the one who calls you. ⁹"A little yeast works through the whole batch of dough." ¹⁰I am confident in the Lord that you will take no other view. The one who is throwing you into confusion will pay the penalty, whoever he may be. ¹¹Brothers, if I am still preaching circumcision, why am I still being persecut-ed? In that case the offense of the cross has been abolished. ¹²As for those agitators, I wish they would go the whole way and emasculate themselves!

*¹³You, my brothers, were called to be free. But do not use your freedom to indulge the sinful nature*ᵃ*; rather, serve one another in love. ¹⁴The entire law is summed up in a sin-gle command: "Love your neighbor as your-self."*ᵇ *¹⁵If you keep on biting and devouring each other, watch out or you will be destroyed by each other.*

Group Questions

TO BEGIN / 15 Minutes (Choose 1 or 2)

❑ In school, how did (do) you feel when others cut in front of you in line? What did (do) you do?
❑ How do you feel and react when others cut in on you in other ways—while driving, shopping, speak-ing, etc.?
❑ Who in this group deserves the award for best hon-oring the commandment—"Love your neighbor as yourself"?

READ SCRIPTURE AND DISCUSS / 30 Minutes

❑ What does Paul mean by a "yoke of slavery" (v. 1)?
❑ Why does Paul make such a big deal about cir-cumcision? Is the practice wrong in and of itself, or only if it is a symbol of the "yoke of slavery"?
❑ Since our own efforts and achievements aren't the way to God, what is (vv. 5–6)?
❑ What spiritual yardstick does your Christian circle use to see who measures up? How does that com-pare to what Paul states in verse 6?
❑ How is Paul's call to serve one another in love (vv. 13–15) reconcilable with his own attitude toward the Judaizers (especially in v. 12!)? How good is Paul at demonstrating "tough love"?
❑ How does Paul balance the area of Christian free-dom—avoiding the extremes of legalistic bondage *and* uncontrolled indulgence (see Note on v. 13)?
❑ How have you seen Christian freedom abused? How do verses 6 and 13 address those who think their freedom in Christ allows them to do anything they want? How do they challenge you?
❑ When have you gotten off the track in the "good race" of the Christian life? Who or what cut in on you and sidetrack you from a childlike faith "expressing itself through love"?
❑ Ironically, though we have been liberated from sla-very, what kind of servants do we become (vv. 13–15)? How good of this kind of servant are you?
❑ Jesus said, "My yoke is easy and my burden is light" (Matt. 11:30). Whose yoke are you wearing—Christ's or your own efforts to win approval?

TO CLOSE AND PRAY / 15–30 Minutes

❑ It's "reality check" time. How are you doing ... *really?*
❑ How would you rate this group in "serving one another in love" versus "biting and devouring each other"? What grade would God give your group?
❑ How can this group pray for the group?
❑ How can this group pray for you?

ᵃ13 Or *the flesh;* also in verses 16,17,19 and 24   ᵇ14 Lev. 19:18

Notes

5:1 Paul sums up the meaning of this allegory: as children of the free woman (4:32), they must tenaciously resist the loss of that freedom.

5:2 *I, Paul.* Paul speaks with the full weight of his apostolic authority. *circumcised.* The removal of the foreskin of the male genital organ, normally on the eighth day after birth. This rite was established by God as a sign of the covenant (Gen. 17).

5:3 If the male members of the church allow themselves to be circumcised (and believe this to be a vital and necessary pat of their salvation), they in essence acknowledge the binding quality of the whole Law over their lives. *lets himself.* An infant has no choice. Others decide to circumcise him. But for adults, it requires a conscious choice to undergo this surgical procedure.

5:4 A person can seek right standing before God either by legal works or by grace—not by both. Grace is not *grace* (a freely given gift) if there is any requirement at all for receiving it. *trying to be justified.* Paul has said repeatedly that it is impossible to gain right standing via the Law (see Rom. 11:7). The only thing the Law brings (in this context) is a curse (3:10–14).

5:5 *Spirit.* It is the Holy Spirit who fosters such assurances of acquittal. *hope.* The Christian can confidently expect a positive verdict on the Judgment Day. To have such a hope *in advance* of the event brings great liberty and rejoicing. This stands in contrast to the anxiety of one who is never sure if he/she has done quite enough "good works" or has been faithful to all points of the Law. Such people (the legalists) will not know until the Last Day if they have made it into God's kingdom.

5:6 *neither circumcision nor uncircumcision.* Neither is a virtue. Christianity has room for all people. Circumcision is the wrong issue. Faith, hope and love (vv. 5–6) are the issues. *faith/love.* Faith is the root, love is the fruit (Bruce).

5:7 *running a good race.* In fact, those who would be most open to the appeals of the Judaizers would be the sincere, dedicated Galatians who wanted nothing more than to please God. But as relatively new Christians, they would not know that they were being diverted into a legalism that led away from Christ.

5:8 If such persuasion does not come from God (who is the one who calls them), the implication is that it comes from Satan (no matter who the agents are).

5:11 Paul replies to the allegation that he is preaching circumcision, a charge that was probably used to convince the Galatians to be circumcised. *abolished.* If a person can earn salvation by circumcision and law-keeping, then a crucified savior is unnecessary (and so the offense and the persecution disappears).

5:12 In a rich (albeit coarse) jibe at the Judaizers, Paul suggests that if they are so preoccupied with circumcision, they really ought to take their knives and make eunuchs out of themselves!

5:13–6:10 In typical fashion, Paul moves from the theological to the practical. His doctrinal case complete, he hastens to show what these truths mean in the life of the believer.

5:13 *free. But ...* What Paul has written about freedom from the Law could be misunderstood to be a license to indulge all one's appetites, and certainly he does not mean that. So he begins this new section on Christian living by examining the use of freedom. What Paul is calling for is responsible freedom, which, as he says, is the freedom to serve others in love. *freedom.* Christian freedom stands between the extreme of legal bondage (life lived within a web of requirements—5:1) and the other extreme of unbridled indulgence (life lived without regard to any rules). Paul has already said that no one can be truly free until Christ takes away his/her burden of guilt (Christ frees a person from the power of the Law). Now he will show that one also needs to be freed from the power of sinful desires, which comes by the infilling of the Holy Spirit. *the sinful nature.* The self-serving, self-seeking, self-indulgent aspect of human nature (see vv. 19–21 for a partial list of its works). *serve.* Literally, serve as slaves. The only form of slavery that is compatible with freedom is self-giving to others.

UNIT 12—Life by the Spirit / Galatians 5:16–26

Scripture

Life by the Spirit

¹⁶So I say, live by the Spirit, and you will not gratify the desires of the sinful nature. ¹⁷For the sinful nature desires what is contrary to the Spirit, and the Spirit what is contrary to the sinful nature. They are in conflict with each other, so that you do not do what you want. ¹⁸But if you are led by the Spirit, you are not under law.

¹⁹The acts of the sinful nature are obvious: sexual immorality, impurity and debauchery; ²⁰idolatry and witchcraft; hatred, discord, jealousy, fits of rage, selfish ambition, dissensions, factions ²¹and envy; drunkenness, orgies, and the like. I warn you, as I did before, that those who live like this will not inherit the kingdom of God.

²²But the fruit of the Spirit is love, joy, peace, patience, kindness, goodness, faithfulness, ²³gentleness and self-control. Against such things there is no law. ²⁴Those who belong to Christ Jesus have crucified the sinful nature with its passions and desires. ²⁵Since we live by the Spirit, let us keep in step with the Spirit. ²⁶Let us not become conceited, provoking and envying each other.

Group Questions

TO BEGIN / 15 Minutes (Choose 1 or 2)

❏ On a scale of 0 (none) to 10 (tons), how many "wild oats" did you sow (are you sowing) in your youth?
❏ Where are you the most pleasant to be around—home, work, school, church, this group, etc.?
❏ Where are you the *least* pleasant to be around?

READ SCRIPTURE AND DISCUSS / 30 Minutes

❏ Over and over Paul has warned the Galatians about being enslaved to legalism. What does he warn them about being enslaved to in this passage?
❏ What two things are in conflict with each other (v. 17)?
❏ What does Paul mean by "live by" ... "led by" ... and "keep in step with" ... the Spirit (vv. 16,18,25; see Note on v. 16)?
❏ If we are made alive by the Spirit, why do we still struggle with sin?
❏ Since we are not under the Law, what is wrong with indulging in our sinful nature once in a while?
❏ Is the list of "acts of the sinful nature" representative or complete? Is anything less than sinless perfection damned, or just sin as a lifestyle (v. 21)? Can a person who lives this way be a true Christian (see Notes on v. 20 and v. 21)?
❏ Is the crucifixion of the sinful nature done *to* the Christian or *by* the Christian (see Note on v. 24)?
❏ Which of the acts of the sinful nature are dead and buried in your life? Which are mortally wounded? Which are alive and well?
❏ Which type of spiritual fruit are blossoming in your life right now? Which are still in the bud?
❏ How can you and God's Spirit kill the first category and grow the second?

TO CLOSE AND PRAY / 15–30 Minutes

❏ Let's do some fruit inspecting ... Listen silently while others in the group identify which aspect of the "fruit of the Spirit" is most evident in your life. Start with one person and go around the circle.
❏ Next week will be the last session in this study. What would you like to do after that? Continue meeting? Multiply into two groups? Have a party to celebrate the time together?
❏ Comparing your present spiritual life and energy to a fruit tree, are you feeling: Young and green, but growing? Robust and productive? Full of wild branches that need to be pruned? Mature but concerned about longevity? Old and tired?
❏ How can your group support you in prayer?

Notes

5:16 Having warned against losing one's freedom by submitting to circumcision (5:1–2), Paul now warns about losing freedom by submitting to sinful desires. *live by the Spirit.* Lit., walk by the Spirit; i.e., let the way you live, your conduct, be directed by the Holy Spirit. It is the Holy Spirit, not the Law, who will bring about a moral lifestyle.

5:17 Two principles are at war in the Christian's life. "But the believer is not the helpless battle group of two opposing forces. If he yields to the flesh, he is enslaved by it, but if he obeys the prompting of the Spirit, he is liberated" (Bruce).

5:18 The Spirit is as opposed to the Law as to the sinful nature (vv. 16–17). To be led by the Spirit enables a person to resist sinful desire. To be under Law, however, gives a person no protection at all against such inner cravings.

5:19 *acts of the sinful nature.* To illustrate specifically the sort of lifestyle that emerges when the sinful nature is allowed its sway, Paul produces a representative list of vices.

5:20 *idolatry.* The worship of any idol, be it a carved image of God (a statue) or an abstract substitute for God (a status symbol). An idol is identified as such because when faced with a choice, a person will follow its leading. Money, for example, becomes an idol when to gain it a person will do anything. *witchcraft.* *Pharmakeia* is literally "the use of drugs," which was often associated with the practice of sorcery.

5:21 *drunkenness.* In the first century, diluted wine was drunk regularly by all ages, but drunkenness was not common and was condemned (because it was thought to turn a person into a beast). *and the like.* The list is representative, not exhaustive—touching, in order, upon the sins of sensuality, idolatry, social dissension, and intemperance. *not inherit.* The issue here is not sins into which one falls, but sin as a lifestyle. These are evidence of a life not controlled by the Spirit, and therefore the implication is that such a person has not been born from above and become a child of God.

5:22–23 In contrast to the "acts of the sinful nature" is the "fruit of the Spirit"—those traits which characterize the child of God. Again, the list is representative and not exhaustive.

5:22 *love.* Agape; in contrast, there is *eros* (sexual love), *philos* (warm feelings to friends and family), and *storge* (family affection). None of these adequately describe the self-giving, active benevolence that is meant to characterize Christian love, hence the repeated use in the NT of *agape*—a relatively uncommon word redefined by Christians to bear this meaning. *peace.* The prime meaning of this word is not negative ("an absence of conflict"), but positive ("the presence of that which brings wholeness and well-being"). *kindness, goodness.* Related words, but whereas *kindness* means the sort of response that is gentle and sweet, *goodness* has to it the added ability to rebuke and discipline when necessary. As Trench points out, Jesus demonstrated *goodness* when he drove the money-changers from the temple, but *kindness* to the harlot who anointed his feet. *self-control.* This is control of one's sensual passions, rather than control of one's anger (as in gentleness). *there is no law.* While it is possible to legislate certain forms of behavior, one cannot command love, joy, peace, etc. These are each gifts of God's grace. With this list of qualities one moves into a whole new realm of reality, well beyond the sphere of Law.

5:24 *have crucified the sinful nature.* It is via the cross that a person dies to the power of the Law (2:19). Paul indicates here that in the same way, a person also dies to the power of their sinful nature. The verb indicates that this is not something done *to* the Christian but *by* the Christian. The Christian actively and deliberately has repented of (turned away from) the old wayward patterns of life.

5:25 *live by the Spirit.* In the same way that the death of the ego (the "I" principle) is replaced by the mind of Christ (2:20), here Paul indicates that the death of the sinful nature is replaced by the life of the Spirit. *let us.* Having just indicated that the Christian does live by the power of the Spirit, Paul (in characteristic fashion) balances off that indicative ("this is the way things are") with an imperative ("now you do this").

UNIT 13—Doing Good to All/Not Circumcision but a New Creation / Galatians 6:1–18

Scripture

Doing Good to All

6 Brothers, if someone is caught in a sin, you who are spiritual should restore him gently. But watch yourself, or you also may be tempted. ²Carry each other's burdens, and in this way you will fulfill the law of Christ. ³If anyone thinks he is something when he is nothing, he deceives himself. ⁴Each one should test his own actions. Then he can take pride in himself, without comparing himself to somebody else, ⁵for each one should carry his own load.

⁶Anyone who receives instruction in the word must share all good things with his instructor.

⁷Do not be deceived: God cannot be mocked. A man reaps what he sows. ⁸The one who sows to please his sinful nature, from that nature^a will reap destruction; the one who sows to please the Spirit, from the Spirit will reap eternal life. ⁹Let us not become weary in doing good, for at the proper time we will reap a harvest if we do not give up. ¹⁰Therefore, as we have opportunity, let us do good to all people, especially to those who belong to the family of believers.

Group Questions

TO BEGIN / 15 Minutes (Choose 1 or 2)

❏ Were you a troublemaker or a peacemaker as a child? In what way?
❏ What kind of garden have you tended? What did you enjoy about it? What did you dread?

READ SCRIPTURE AND DISCUSS / 30 Minutes

❏ How do verses 1–2 illustrate ways of helping someone to "keep in step with the Spirit" (5:25)? What is the "law of Christ" (see 5:14)?
❏ How can you restore a fellow Christian caught in sin, and avoid feeling superior to that person or being tempted by the same sin?
❏ How does verse 5 relate to verse 2 (see Notes on v. 2 and v. 5)? Are they contradictory? What sorts of burdens do your friends carry? How do you (or could you) help them with these burdens?
❏ What is the gist of Paul's teaching on the Spirit-filled life (vv. 7–10)? Where in your life do you need to sow to please the Spirit?
❏ How does Paul sum up the motives of the false teachers (vv. 12–13)? His own motives (v. 14)? How concerned are you about creating a good outward impression? Is your concern greater or lesser than it used to be? Why?
❏ What does it mean to have the cross as your model in daily life? What does it mean to "boast" in the cross of Jesus? Is this boasting a part of your life? In what way, or how would you like it to be?
❏ Ultimately, why is keeping the Jewish rules irrelevant? From elsewhere in Galatians, how would you describe what the "new creation" (v. 15) is all about?
❏ Why does Paul call these Gentile Galatians the "Israel of God" (v. 16; see 3:6–9)? How is that a final rebuke to those who would compel these believers to obey Jewish rules?
❏ What does Paul mean by bearing on his body the marks of Jesus (v. 17; see 2 Cor. 11:23–30)? Why would Paul's willingness to suffer be a further rebuke to the false teachers? Do you bear any "marks of Jesus"?

[Scripture and questions continued on page 62]

---

^{a}8 Or *his flesh, from the flesh*

Notes

6:1–2 Paul immediately applies what he taught in 5:13–26, beginning with the case of a church member who has given in to temptation. Contrary to what some might expect, he does not counsel harshness but rather burden-bearing love.

6:1 *a sin.* A temporary lapse (as over against an active lifestyle). *you who are spiritual.* Those whose lives bear the mark of the Spirit. This is not a clique of "special" Christians but is the call to all Christians (5:24–25). *restore.* A medical term, used to describe the setting of a fractured bone. The verb tense (in Greek) implies that this is not a single act but a continuous action. *gently.* This is a fruit of the Spirit (v. 23). The temptation may be to display overt disapproval and censorious judgement on the offender, but Paul counsels otherwise. *watch yourself.* No one is beyond temptation; all are vulnerable, so no one has any basis for self-righteousness. To watch means not simply to glance casually, but to gaze with concentration (such as an archer concentrating on a target prior to loosing an arrow). This is active self-examination. This concept is picked up again in verse 4 in the idea of testing one's actions.

6:2 This is the general principle which lies behind the specific instruction in verse 1. *carry each other's burdens.* Mutual burden-bearing lies at the heart of Christian fellowship. *burdens.* A heavy, crushing weight which a single individual cannot carry. *law of Christ.* The law of love (5:14), which stands in sharp contrast to the Law as practiced in first-century Israel. It involves submission to a *person* (Jesus), not to a *code* (the Law of Moses).

6:3 A warning against spiritual pride. A sense of self-importance would make it difficult for such a person to bear another's burden (much less to restore gently the person overtaken in sin).

6:4 *each one should test.* This is an individual act. There is no "committee on standards" set up to evaluate individual Christians. The word for *test* is the same one used to describe the testing of metals to see if they are pure. *his own actions.* The subject of the self-assessment is not inner feelings or ideological commitments, but measurable activity. The question is: how is my life being lived? Note also that it is one's own actions, not those of other people, that are to be examined. *without comparing.* The temptation is to say, "Oh, I'm not so bad. Look at what so-and-so does," thus deflecting true insight into oneself and giving rise to false pride.

6:5 *load.* This is not the same as the crushing burden in verse 2. Rather, the word is used to describe the small individual pack a hiker or soldier carries. This is the same word used by Jesus in Matthew 11:30 to describe the burden (load) of his yoke.

6:6 As an example of burden-bearing in action, Paul cites the obligation of the church to support its teachers (Matt. 10:10; 1 Cor. 9:14). The instructor lifts the burden of ignorance and misunderstanding from the shoulders of the congregation, while they in turn share in the material support of the teacher (lifting his/her burden to provide daily sustenance).

6:7 *mocked.* This is derived from the word for "snout," and means "to turn up one's nose" at somebody in contempt.

6:8–9 "What the apostle is saying is that if we base our lives on the principle that self comes first we shall end up, rotten to the core, in spiritual death. If we let the Spirit of Jesus guide our behavior, the end-product is life as God meant it to be, life lived in such a relationship to God that the death of the body cannot destroy it" (Neil).

6:9 *give up.* That is, lose heart. The idea is of fatigue, such as laborers in the field might feel under the blazing sun. Still they must keep on gathering in the harvest.

6:11 Paul takes pen in hand and writes the final paragraph of his letter, having dictated it up to this point. He calls attention to this, because his letter would most likely be read aloud to the church and people would not see for themselves the change in handwriting. *large letters.* For emphasis' sake, probably.

6:12 *avoid being persecuted.* The motivation behind the Judaizers is self-interest. If they can persuade the Gentile Christians to be circumcised, they will avoid reprisals by the militants in Jerusalem (see Note on 2:12). *for the cross of Christ.* To these zealots, the cross was offensive, since it excluded the need for the Law of Moses.

[Notes continued on page 63]

Scripture (Continued)

Not Circumcision but a New Creation

[11]See what large letters I use as I write to you with my own hand!

[12]Those who want to make a good impression outwardly are trying to compel you to be circumcised. The only reason they do this is to avoid being persecuted for the cross of Christ. [13]Not even those who are circumcised obey the law, yet they want you to be circumcised that they may boast about your flesh. [14]May I never boast except in the cross of our Lord Jesus Christ, through which[b] the world has been crucified to me, and I to the world. [15]Neither circumcision nor uncircumcision means anything; what counts is a new creation. [16]Peace and mercy to all who follow this rule, even to the Israel of God.

[17]Finally, let no one cause me trouble, for I bear on my body the marks of Jesus.

[18]The grace of our Lord Jesus Christ be with your spirit, brothers. Amen.

Group Questions (Continued)

TO CLOSE AND PRAY / 15–30 Minutes

❏ In what way has God greatly inspired or convicted you through your study of Galatians?

❏ How has this group contributed to what God has done in your life through this study?

❏ What have you appreciated about each person in the group? Take turns sharing about one person at a time.

❏ Would you like to continue with this group in a new study? What would you want to change if the group continues? What should stay the same? (See also page 4.)

❏ How has your prayer life changed as a result of being in this group? What would you like the group to remember in prayer for you in the coming weeks?

[b]14 Or *whom*

Notes (Continued)

6:13 The concern of the Judaizers is not just "zeal for the Lord" (as they might protest), but so that they can boast of the many that follow their teaching. **obey the law.** Paul is probably not pointing a finger at specific examples of law-breaking on their part, but at the impossibility for anyone to keep the Law.

6:14 boast ... in the cross. To both Jew and Greek, a cross was a symbol of horror. Polite Romans would not even mention it, and orthodox Jews saw it as a sign of God's curse. But this is what Paul boasts in! **the world.** The world system of values, ideas and powers that is opposed to God. **crucified to me.** Paul is dead to the influence of these anti-God ideas and powers. The crucifixion of Christ has become the pattern on which his life is based (2:20).

6:15 new creation. While the full benefits and extent of this new creation will be experienced only in the age to come, believers experience it in part here and now, through the Holy Spirit.

6:17 marks of Jesus. In contrast to the now meaningless mark of circumcision (v. 15a), Paul bears scars as a result of his service for Christ. An example of this would be from the stoning at Lystra (Acts 14:19), which Paul's readers would have known about (since this letter was addressed to the church there). In the first century, slaves were branded with their owner's mark. In a real sense, Paul is the slave of Christ. In certain pagan cults, devotees were tattooed to show to whom they belonged.

6:18 Paul ends with a warm, personal note. His anger is done with. He has said what must be said. He concludes by recalling their common kinship in Christ.

ACKNOWLEDGEMENTS

The central source consulted for the Notes in this study was F. F. Bruce's *Commentary on Galatians* (New International Greek Testament Series), Grand Rapids, MI: Wm. B. Eerdmans Publishing Co., 1982. In addition, good use was made of *The Letter of Paul to the Galatians* (The Cambridge Bible Commentary) by William Neil (Cambridge: The University Press, 1967) and *Galatians* (The New Century Bible Commentary series) by Donald Guthrie (Grand Rapids, MI: Wm. B. Eerdmans Publishing Co., 1981). Reference was also made to *Only One Way: The Message of Galatians* (The Bible Speaks Today series) by John R.W. Stott (Downers Grove, IL: InterVarsity Press, 1968); *Galatians* (*Hermeneia*) by Hans Dieter Betz (Philadelphia: Fortress Press, 1979); *2 Corinthians and Galatians* (Neighborhood Bible Studies) by Marilyn Kunz and Catherine Schell (Wheaton, IL: Tyndale House Publishers, 1975); and *St. Paul's Epistle to the Galatians,* by J. B. Lightfoot (Grand Rapids, MI: Zondervan); as well as to the standard lexicons, dictionaries, etc.